WITNESS

TO TWO

WORLDS

A MEMOIR OF
BIPOLAR DISORDER,
IMMIGRATION,
AND FATIH

WITNESS

TO TWO

WORLDS

A MEMOIR OF BIPOLAR DISORDER, IMMIGRATION, AND FATIH

Giovanna Campomizzi May

Erminia "My Angel" Publishing
Rochester, NY

Cover design and layout by Nina Alvarez of Dream Your Book

For permission to reprint portions of this book,
or to order a review copy, contact:
giovannamay47@gmail.com

ISBN-13: 978-0-578-68567-0

CONTENTS

DISCLAIMER

The names of many of the characters in this memoir have been changed and some conversations have been altered, but the incidents described are true and actually did take place. What is stated in this book is factual to the best of my recollection.

DEDICATION

I dedicate this book to my husband, Bill, who always helps me during my good and bad days, and to my children and their children. They help me to live with this disease every day by loving me as I am.

I also dedicate this book to the millions of people who suffer from bipolar disorder. I understand their agony because I have walked and continue to walk in their shoes.

I cannot skip devoting this book to my mother and father who are both deceased. They dedicated their lives to my sister Lucy and me so that we could follow our dreams.

Whatever, wherever I am, I can never be thrown away. If I am in sickness, my sickness may serve Him; in perplexity, my perplexity may serve Him; If I am in sorrow, my sorrow may serve Him. He does nothing in vain. He knows what He is about. He may take away my friends, He may throw me among strangers, He may make me feel desolate, may make my spirits sink, hide my future from me—still He knows what He is about. Therefore, I will trust Him.

— from "A Meditation" by Cardinal John Newman

PREFACE

This book is not intended to be a textbook about the disease of bipolar disorder. Many very good and informative books have been written that discuss the characteristics and symptoms of this illness.

This is the story of my life and how it has been affected by this disorder. It is a true story. I use my own name and the names of my family and friends. I have changed the names of many of the others who appear in the book to protect them.

Of course, my name is confusing. My birth name is Giovanna Campomizzi. When I came to America, it was changed to Joann Campomizzi. When I married, it became Joann Campomizzi May. When I was fifty, I decided to return to my roots and changed my name back to Giovanna. My name is now legally Giovanna Campomizzi May.

I have benefitted from writing this book and I hope that those who read it, especially those who suffer from bipolar disorder, will be comforted by my story.

Giovanna Campomizzi May
Rochester, New York
February 2020

INTRODUCTION

I really started writing this book many, many years ago while I was under the care of my psychiatrist, Dr. Lyman Wynne. He asked me to keep a journal. I continued through the years that followed, recording my ups and downs. About fifteen years ago, I decided to write a book about this illness and my life. I also decided to change my name legally from Joann back to Giovanna.

My writing began with the journal entries, which led to my medical records. They were a good starting point and provided a wealth of information, events that kindled the memory of what really happened over the course of more than thirty years. I was able to recall details, relive moments that had a profound impact over the course of my life. The happy times included my marriage, the birth of our children, and a career in teaching. The memories also brought with them the dark side that I wanted to forget, but couldn't. The stigma of my illness left me afraid and guilt-ridden most of my life. But I needed to find the link between my behavior and my illness; I wanted to know when it began and, if possible, how.

This is a difficult time in my life to talk about, to relive, to remember.

When I was a young girl, my father told me about his memories of some of the horrors he had seen during World War II. I could hear his words. I could believe him. He was my father. But the words did not make sense. I tried to understand what simply could not be possible. Yet he said that it was true, and it was.

The following feels something like encountering these memories of my father's, except that now the struggle was within me, a battle for my own sanity. I knew there was a real world where I lived with my husband and children. I believed that they and my faith sustained me. I sensed that out there life went on with its entirely hectic and bumpy normalcy, but I could not reach any of it. I felt as if I were being dragged into another world where my own judgment was being trumped by anxiety and fear. And the terrifying part of this is that I could not rely on my own judgment to tell me this. Others had to confront me with an illness that denies its own existence.

I relate these events through my own memories, patient records, and the accounts of others who experienced my illness from their own perspective. In the end, all I can hope—for the intensity of feeling is beyond the power of words—is to leave an impression of a fall from rational thought into an egocentric black hole and the patience and persistence of those who stayed with me.

PART ONE:

BEFORE THE FALL

CHAPTER 1

A SEARING, FURIOUS NOW

Somewhere deep inside, I knew there was something very wrong with me. I had no conception of time. Everything was a searing, furious now. In the midst of the nightmare, the terror intensified. How would my husband and kids feel if they saw me like this?

The previous May, I had earned my master's degree. Fewer than three months later, I was locked up in isolation in the psychiatric wing of a hospital.

I remember pushing the call button on the wall repeatedly just to harass the nurses. When one arrived, I would remain motionless on the mattress until she approached me. Then I would scream and jump from the mattress to the floor, flailing, ordering her to let me see my husband and my children. Sometimes I would make a run for the door. I didn't get very far. I refused to listen to anything anyone said. I insisted there was nothing wrong with me.

Around what seemed to be midmorning I was given a shot of Haldol, an antipsychotic drug to calm patients under severe mental duress. I continued this routine, up and down, pounding and screaming, eventually collapsing facedown on the mattress. About an hour later, I received another dose of Haldol. I tried to force my way out of the room. More Haldol. This time I refused it.

Two more nurses burst through the door with a gurney. Held by all fours, I screamed, panted, wrestled to free myself, demanded to be heard. The staff ushered me onto the gurney and strapped my hands and feet to the rails. My eyes darted from nurse to nurse, glaring with contempt. I fought the restraints as one of them gave me the shot of Haldol. The straps—I remember they were white—felt like they were made of fur. I was overheating. Torture. I struggled against the sheets with my arms and legs.

Through the next ten hours I became more manipulative, manic, and paranoid. I thrashed and fought the restraints, screaming until I was utterly exhausted. Then I would drift into a coma of sleep for an hour or so, wake up, and begin the battle all over again, ridiculing the nurse on watch with me, fighting with everything I had to be free of the restraints.

> *God, where are you? Do you see what they are doing to me? Why don't you stop them? Is this your plan for my life? Am I supposed to accept all this disgrace? Do I have a choice?*

I was given several more doses of Haldol, orally when I would take them, more often by injection when I spit the oral dose out. I hurled my head up and down on the mattress, cursing the nurses, ordering them again and again not to hurt my baby, raging that I was being raped, insisting that there was nothing wrong with me. Eventually I managed to work my hands free. Nurses resecured the restraints and taped my hands down for good measure. An hour later, I worked my hands free again, and again, they had to be taped back down.

I fought the body restraints, flat out on a gurney, barely able to move, and still I fell and kept falling. I could not free myself.

By 10 p.m., after hours of restraint and many doses of Haldol, I had apparently calmed down enough to be freed from the gurney. A nurse escorted me back to my bedroom. I pounded on the door for as long as I could then toppled down, exhausted.

Somewhere deep inside I kept asking: *How do I escape from me?*

CHAPTER 2

VIA AEILLA

As a very young girl in Italy, my maternal grandfather, Papa Domenico, would tell stories of America. He would sit backwards on a chair outside the front door of his house, sometimes reminiscing over evenings come and gone, other times reading a copy of *Life* magazine or an American newspaper he subscribed to. There were times I played with my sister; there were times he told us stories; there were times he read or remembered, and I would look at the mountains around our village and wonder about how big this little world of mine was.

And there were times when I sat with him alone. He would smile at me with his eyes the color of stonewashed jeans, through glasses with lenses as thick as a magnifying glass, and tell me of a land across the sea — a land of cities that sprouted and grew like fields of grain, of buildings that reached as high into the sky as the rocky outcrops of our little village, a place so big that our whole country could fit into one of its states, and it had forty-eight of them.

"America is a land, Giovanna," he so often said, "where anyone can make their dreams come true if they are willing to get an education and work hard." He would puff on his pipe, sip his homemade red wine, and dream an old man's dreams. Of days that had been, and of days to come.

Perched in the Apennine Mountains in the province of L'Aquila, Aielli is a small, peaceful village of a few hundred people with a panoramic view of the countryside below. This peace, as well as the care of many family members, helped shape me. My extended family on both sides was quite large: maternal grandparents, six aunts (my mother had only sisters), five uncles, and seven cousins. Besides the relatives on my mom's side of the family, I also had many aunts, uncles, and cousins on my father's side.

My parents gave me the name Giovanna Campomizzi, after my paternal grandfather, Giovanni Campomizzi. I was his first grandchild. Although I was not a boy—very important to that generation—my parents, aunts, uncles, cousins, and all four grandparents gave me an enormous welcome.

I enjoyed two worlds from the start: that of my mother's family and that of my father's family. My father had two brothers and three sisters, *zia* and *zio,* Italian for *aunt* and *uncle.* All of them, except my Zia Lucia who lived in America, lived in Aielli. My father had been born in Flushing, Ohio. The rest of the children were born in Aielli. His family had lived in America until he was four, then they returned to Aielli and lived exceptionally well on the money Papa Giovanni had made working on the railroads.

My father left for America one frigid February morning in 1952. Dressed in our winter clothes, we made the ten-minute walk down the mountain to the edge of town and the gray stone train station. Papa smoked as he spoke quietly with Mamma. She carried Lucia in her arms. I walked alongside them. My father's two brothers marched a few steps behind, carrying the suitcase and trunk he was taking with him. Beneath a brilliant blue sky we waved goodbye as he found a seat, smiled, and waved back through a window. I was excited for my father as the train left for Naples. We all tried to pretend that nothing had changed as we returned to Papa Domenico's house. We Italians are very good at ignoring the unpleasant. I had no idea how much I would miss him. Two years was a long, long time.

Family did its best to fill the void. Mamma taught us, with her father's resolve, the difference between right and wrong and the joys of working the land. Farming was our way of life. A couple of my aunts stayed at my Papa Domenico's house with the youngest children. My mother and the rest of her sisters walked me the couple of miles to their father's fields. At the age of four, I was one of several children old enough to go.

They used mules and cows to pull plows over acres of land and, after planting, used hoes and shovels to till the furrows along with hired workers. I can still see mother's blue-and-white-checkered scarf wrapped around her head to help keep away the heat, and her constantly wiping the sweat over her forehead with a towel as she baled hay. I played in the dirt and dug up small pieces of colored glass with my hands. I remember rubbing off the dirt and looking at the hot sun reflecting off the glass.

Working on the farm was not my mother's only skill. She also made her own material on a large loom by throwing the shuttle between the long threads and working it to make cloth. Her work fascinated and entertained me. I often sat on her lap in front of the loom, mesmerized by the action of the shuttle. My mother made me happy. The cotton thread used in the loom, too coarse for clothing, created the linens for our home.

At sixteen, mother had graduated with honors from a dress designing school in Avezzano, a nearby city. She was talented at designing clothes and made men's suits, women's dresses and suits, children's clothing, and most of the clothes we wore. Aielli did not have a fabric store. Four or five times a year, she would make the hour ride by train to Avezzano to buy material. In the midst of working the farm, weaving, and making our clothes, Mamma also had to make time each day for the five-minute trip to the piazza. She held Lucia in one arm and led me by the other while she balanced a water pail on her head, which she used to fetch the water we needed for the day. The women of the town kneaded their own dough at home for bread but took it to the communal brick oven in the town square for baking, one more journey for her several times a week.

Despite these joyful memories, there was something else beneath the hot summer sun of Italy: an oppressive absence that longed to be filled. Seed planted in March, nourished by warmth and rain, sprouted, drank the sun, flourished, filled the fields, but couldn't fill the emptiness. It hung in the air like the heat. I wondered if my mother could read my mind, could feel my loneliness, could know the ghost inside of me, somewhere beyond reach. Many days, so many days, I daydreamed about my father. When he left, he took a part of us with him. Living in the upstairs apartment of his parents' house, it was as if a part of him still walked the rooms in a world I couldn't see, calling us to tomorrows I couldn't imagine.

I remember a day in September 1952, harvest season in Italy. Mamma was working in the wheat fields, ripe for harvesting, using a sickle to form the wheat into bales with the help of her sisters and the laborers hired by my grandfather. She was agile and strong. Strands of chestnut-brown hair fell from her scarf as her lean shoulders swung to the rhythm of the work. I knew the rhythm of the leather high-top boots knotted at the knees beneath her dress as she made her routine stops to where I played. She would smile from the depths of her hazel eyes and hand me a bit of something to eat from the knapsack she carried to the fields each day. Sometimes she would cut her hand with a sickle and would use wine to wash away the blood. I admired my mother.

At midday we would take a break from the heat and make the long walk to my grandparents' house for lunch. After the noonday sun had passed, the adults would return to the fields. My sister, cousins, and I would take naps on small beds in the upstairs rooms. Everyone left the fields around five in the afternoon. The three of us routinely ate supper at Mamma Erminia and Papa Domenico's before returning to my father's house for the night.

Papa Giovanni and Mamma Victoria, my father's parents, were more laid back. They tended to take life with a drizzle of honey rather than a grain of salt, flowing from one event to another. In some way I could never understand, they seemed to ride destiny trusting that whatever happened, things would be okay.

We spent many hours at my maternal grandparents' house with its host of relatives. My maternal aunts and uncles spent an enormous amount of time with us. I remember my favorite uncle, Zio Guido, who liked to play tricks on me. I loved to dance around the house, through the kitchen, across the chairs, anywhere, when delight got its hands on me. At times, Zio Guido would stop me in the kitchen.

"Do you want an orange?" He sat at our big wooden table with a bare-wood bench on one side and rustic chairs on the other. Short and built as powerful as a plow horse, he put down his knife with a smile as he offered me the orange. I giggled, danced over to him, and reached out.

"Here, have one." My uncle had meticulously peeled an orange, taken out the fruit, and put the peel back together. It fell apart in my hands. He chuckled the chuckle I came to love and would encourage me to continue dancing on the table in Papa Domenico's kitchen, which I joyfully did.

The huge room was a welcoming place and always bustled with activity. Everyone was busy except for my grandmother, Mamma Erminia. She had a heart condition and only smiled, or spoke to us with few words. My cousins Gaetano, Benedetto, and Rosina and my sister Lucia were also there. Rosina was a year older than I and much nicer to me than my male cousins. She often wanted us to go play with our dolls and leave the boys to their own fun. Benedetto was only three, my sister's age. They played side by side. Lucia was a real pro at cracking almonds and giving them to my grandfather. Benedetto would help her.

"Lucia, Benedetto, crack one of those almonds for me and I'll give you a kiss."

They'd give him the almonds and he would reach in his jacket pocket and give them a Hershey's Kiss.

During the freezing weather, my cousins and I held our hands over the fire in the fireplace in order to stay warm. Black iron hooks of various sizes hung around the fireplace to hold pots and pans. I can still see my aunts boiling potatoes in a huge pot and roasting chestnuts in a pan over the fire, with my bossy cousin Gaetano standing by the fire.

"Move over," he would say with a shove. "I want to warm up." I listened to him, partly out of fear. "Here, eat the crust off my bread. I don't like it." I would eat the crust off the bread and hand it back to him.

Self-conscious even as a young child, I would obey. I remembered my manners; I wondered why he didn't. Many times, someone cooking at the hearth would ask me if I wanted a piece of potato from one of the pots. I did not know how not to say "please."

We grew our own crops and raised our own livestock, mostly cows, hogs, and chickens. They provided meat that we roasted in the fireplace and eggs. At the breakfast table, Mamma would mix sugar and a touch of Marsala wine with beaten raw eggs. Lucia and I would willingly drink them. If we went out to the barn, she would gather eggs, poke a small hole in one end and a larger one in the other, and have us suck the egg from the shell. I lived on raw eggs for breakfast until I was fourteen years old and living in America.

The house was built of stone and stucco and stayed cool even during the hot summer days. We would stay inside the huge kitchen for a couple of hours. A huge hearth stood in the middle of the kitchen and served as the hub of all family functions. Made of large gray stones of various sizes reaped from years of tilling the mountain soil, the fireplace served us in all seasons as both heater and stove. To one side a staircase led to the small bedrooms upstairs; to the other, two steps led to the door of Papa Domenico's wine cellar, my sister Lucia's favorite place to sit.

Wine is a mainstay of Italian life. Italy routinely ranks as the largest producer of wine in the world. The cultivation of vineyards and wine-making on the Italian peninsula predate the Roman Empire. It is a tradition deeply woven into the fabric of Italian culture, and my family was devoted to the custom. My grandfather's pride and joy was his wine cellar. Down the two steps next to the fireplace resided the inner sanctum where he made and stored his wine. With the fall harvest came the grapes he would crush in his cellar while wearing heavy black rubber boots that reached to his thighs. Always a busy man during the harvest, he found time to strain, barrel, and ferment the quantity needed to last until the next harvest, enough for the family and enough for a couple of glasses of wine each day for the laborers at lunch. I'm not sure what the total quantity was.

I tell this tale from the annals of history as a story told to me, for I never saw the inside of the wine cellar. My mother's side of the family was firmly held under the rule of Papa Domenico, the patriarch who commanded what each family member from the oldest to the youngest would do and think. He was barely 5'7" but when he walked into a room, we knew he was there. We respected him and no one ever thought to disobey him.

"Children, do not come into my wine cellar," he always reminded us, with a tone of voice that resembled Divine Authority.

He drank at least a liter of wine a day and lived to be eighty-six.

I was blessed and never lacked for attention, but no one could replace my father. Part of the daily routine was our little family's stroll to the piazza to meet and talk and play with other families doing the same thing. Papa held Lucia and led me by the hand as Mamma chatted with neighbors along the way. When my father left for America, my dad's younger brother, Zio Luigi, took over the family rituals. There were times when I noticed my hand in his and looked up. Seeing my uncle reminded me of my father and made the missing worse. Nevertheless, the joys of these early years would sustain me in coping with life once we moved to America.

At the age of three, I began attending the local nursery school. The school was located inside a large brick building that was in the center of our village near the piazza. Catholic nuns taught us how to read and write. We learned how to use a needle and thread, pencils, and scissors, how to cut up an apple into thin slices with a small knife — practical skills. They encouraged our independence, and I loved learning. I moved on to kindergarten and could read fluently in Italian by the age of five.

When we entered first grade at the age of six, we were required to wear uniforms. The boys' and girls' were the same colors. The girls wore black gabardine wool jumpers and white cotton blouses with large round Peter Pan collars and long cuffed sleeves. The boys wore black wool dress pants with a white long-sleeved shirt, a black tie, and a black knit vest. I loved wearing my uniform and I loved attending school. I was overjoyed in the classroom. We sat at heavy brown wooden desks with holes cut out in the top for ink bottles. The paired desks were arranged in neat rows. I sat next to one of my friends, Marina, who was always trying to get me in trouble but never succeeded. I had a keen curiosity and desire for knowledge. Oh, how I loved to learn in the little classroom.

One morning my behavior changed clear out of the blue. I can think of no good reason why. I woke up and ate my raw egg for breakfast as usual. My mother was dressing me for school when some feeling, something I still cannot describe, came over me.

"I don't want to go to school today!" I screamed.

"You have to." My aunt and mother worked together to get my coat on me and tried to push me out the door. I resisted, but they won.

"I want my father!" I felt the tears flowing down my face. I felt the pain, something like a rage toward my mother, as if she were the one who convinced him to go away.

They literally dragged me toward school. I was still screaming and kicking my feet by the time we reached the piazza. My mother held me and tried to calm me down. She could not control the outbursts and finally gave up.

"I want my father!" The tears and the tantrum continued.

"Your father is in America." She struggled to quiet me down but did not succeed. I spent the morning drifting between bouts of crying and a sanctuary of silence.

That afternoon, in our apartment at Papa Giovanni's house, I eventually cried myself to exhaustion and fell asleep until the next morning.

The next day I eagerly went to school, but these temper tantrums intensified and grew in strength. I have vivid memories of yelling at my mother and strongly disagreeing with her on a daily basis. Every time, she would question my behavior and ask me to stop. Eventually, after wearing myself out, I would stop.

Finally, January 1954 arrived, and within weeks we would leave for America and see my father. In November 1953, my sister and I had been fitted for new dresses and measured for new shoes in Papa Domenico's kitchen. Our aunts Genovefa and Mimma were making us three new dresses each for our long journey. The shoemaker in town made us each a pair of brown leather high-top shoes. I could hardly wait to wear them; the dresses were tailored, classic in style. Mine had pleats in the front and were a lighter brown than my shoes. Lucia's dresses, the same color as mine, were gathered and smocked in the front and back.

My anticipation grew. I couldn't wait to be with my father again. When my mother, my sister, and I finally left Aielli, I didn't know I would not see my relatives again for decades. I did not comprehend what I was leaving behind.

CHAPTER 3

THE *ANDREA DORIA*

On January 22, 1954, we left Aielli from the same train station as my father did two years before. My aunts, uncles, and cousins walked to the station with us to see us off and say goodbye. My mother's father and two of her sisters were coming with us to Naples. At that time, a family immigrating to America was as common an occurrence as the handful of others boarding on their way to their daily affairs. I sat at a window seat next to my mother and sister, my grandfather and aunts across the aisle, and gazed out across the plateau to the mountains beyond.

I was jubilant as the train pulled away from the station for the three-hour trip to Naples. I had never been on a long train ride before, and this was the beginning of the journey that would bring me to my father. As the train clattered over the rails, pine trees seemed to reach out to us. Houses and farms that clung to mountain slopes slipped behind us as we made our way to the southern coast. Clusters of small settlements stained gray by winter hugged valleys strung with rows upon rows of barren grapevines waiting for the warmth of spring. Fields and pastures dotted with sheep, goats, and cows rose and fell with the hills as we passed and disappeared into an Italy as ancient as the trails through the mountains. As the train hurtled along the main road south that skirted the rail line, billboards shuffled past the windows like a magician flipping cards. I was old enough to know how to read. Papa Domenico encouraged me to read the billboards aloud—Ravioli Latticini Freschi, Pyrex Glamorama, Birra Italia Pilsen, and Pizza Italiana—giving me a Hershey's Kiss for each one I managed. The speed of the train made the game a real challenge. I couldn't wait to be able to read in English.

There were stretches along the way when my mind would

wander, hypnotized by the rhythm of the steel wheels on the tracks and the rumpled familiarity of the terrain. It was Lucia's third birthday, but we didn't celebrate her actual birth date. Italian custom instead celebrates the feast day of the Catholic saint someone is named after, so we had celebrated her birthday on December 13, the feast of Saint Lucy.

Four days before we left was my father's birthday. Although he was born in America, he grew up in Italy and married my mother, a girl from his hometown, in 1946. Six years later, when he was thirty years old, he returned to the United States to prepare a home for my mother, my sister, and me. Papa Domenico had frowned upon the marriage of his daughter to my father. But he made all the arrangements for our trip and now he was sitting a few seats away, on his way to Naples with our little family and my mother's sisters, to see us off.

When we arrived in Naples, I took my first ride on a bus to our hotel. In Aielli during the winter months, we had hot stones like embers in a little metal cage in our bed. My mother pushed the cage to the bottom of the bed between the top and bottom sheets. The stones radiated enough heat to keep us warm for an entire night. In the hotel room, we slept in beds with no stones in them. We were not accustomed to cold sheets touching our feet. It was the beginning of many changes.

The next day, we took a bus from our hotel to the port of Naples to get a look at our ship. We found her, the *Andrea Doria*, and marveled at her size and majestic features. At 700 feet long, she was longer than the center of our little town and would carry more than one thousand passengers across the Atlantic on our voyage. Her razor-thin bow flared out to the breadth of her jet-black hull, capped with a white superstructure and one graceful funnel banded at the top in deep green, white, and red, the colors of the Italian flag. Her decks alone rose more than a hundred feet above the waterline, taller than the buildings around her. Sleek and beautiful, just a year out from her maiden voyage, she looked to me to be the biggest and most beautiful creation I had ever seen, an elegant city that sailed the sea. I was jubilant to think that we would be boarding her for seven wonderful days. I could hardly wait.

The next day, a cold spell swept down the mountains, spilling across the harbor. A chill crept into our new adventure. I was six years old, not much more than three feet tall, clinging to my grandfather's arm in the midst of a surge of humanity — passengers, well-wishers, dockworkers, and port officials. Little could dampen the thrill for me — I was too young to understand — but I could feel the sorrow of Papa Domenico, Zia Genovefa, and Zia Maria like I could feel the chill of the air. And I could see the sadness in their smiles.

My mother said her final goodbyes. "I don't know when I'll see you again." She cried softly but more deeply than when she said goodbye to my father.

When I look back on that day, it was as if a sorrow conceived in her when my father left for America had come full term, a sorrow that would remain with her. A sorrow that she handed to her sisters and her father as she took Lucia from Maria's arms into her own. She turned and looked at the huge ship, then back into her father's eyes as she slipped my hand from his into hers.

"I'll miss you very much." She began to sob uncontrollably as she kissed her father and sisters goodbye. No one knew what to say.

For a long moment, amid the noise of boarding passengers, the howl of machines loading cargo, the crew directing the commerce of crossing the Atlantic, all I could hear was the silence. Our hour had come. My grandfather and aunts gave us a final hug and told us that Jesus would take care of us. Mamma turned to Lucia and me.

"May God grant us many blessings."

We turned and headed for the ship.

The history of a family is a history of choices — decisions made by individuals that in ways small or profound alter its destiny for generations. Within families are gossip and funny stories, tales of tenderness and sorrow, attractions, delights, and regrets. Some become the stuff of legend. So it was with Papa Domenico, who left for America just before World War I to build a new life for his family. He joined the army to fight for the United States, returning to Italy after the war because his wife was too sick to make the journey to the States. And now he was choosing to send us to our father in America. He stood near the *Andrea Doria* that day — short, powerfully built in a gray suit, white shirt, and tie, his grayish blond hair thinning with the years, as courageous as ever — watching his daughter and his two granddaughters embark on the same journey he had made nearly forty years earlier. Papa Domenico, who, more than anyone else, instilled in me a strong sense of truth and patriotism, stood in silence, as strong as the mountains that bred him.

The officials ordered us to board the ship. We stepped into the line of passengers ready to board the extra-wide wooden gangway that led to the entrance of the ship. A thick rope railing to keep us from falling off on either side connected fifty or more posts. They had been fastened to planks that were the footbridge between the dock and the ship. Mamma held Lucia in her left arm, our tickets in her left hand, as I walked beside her.

"Look out, Lucia, you will fall into the water." Mother clutched Lucia closer, who was trying to throw a small green pocketknife into the water. My father had given it to my mother as a good luck charm for her journey. Mamma blocked the attempt and Lucia continued to amuse herself with it.

The family we were leaving behind lingered until we reached the ship's entrance. We waved back and forth through a silent dialogue of smiles and tears. Papa Domenico, Zia Genovefa, and Zia Maria turned to leave. I glanced through the railings and the throngs of people. My mother's family grew smaller and smaller as they walked down the pier for their bus. We stepped on board into a mass of hundreds and hundreds of mothers and fathers, children and babies, old and young, and began looking for our cabin. Mamma towed us along the main deck searching numbered and lettered passageways for the one that would take us to our room.

Once on board, she put Lucia down. I helped to take care of

her, holding her hand, talking to her, singing to her. My sister seemed utterly at ease with our new adventure. We worked our way down three decks through thinning streams of passengers, searching staircases and hallways, Lucia in her new dress with the pocketknife in tow behind me in my new dress, in tow behind Mother in a navy blue skirt and blazer, white blouse, a gold necklace, and matching earrings. We wandered from passageway to passageway, from guide to guide, trying to find our cabin. When we finally found our quarters, Mamma picked up Lucia as she unlocked the door. I couldn't wait. I was the first through.

I felt my dreams of America, the land of the rich, the glee of our new adventure, drain from my smile. The room was very small, with a set of bunk beds along one wall, a narrow stretch of floor, a single bed along the other, and a small sink in a corner. Mamma caught the look on my face.

"It's tourist class," she said. My mother had just said goodbye to her family and was about to set out with us on a journey to America and a husband she had not seen for two years. She seemed to be genuinely excited to manage it all and saw the disappointment on my face as an affront to her efforts. She heaved the suitcase onto the bed. "In no time, we'll make it like home."

We unpacked our clothes and put them neatly in our small drawers. Mamma lined up enough underwear for my sister and me for seven days. I looked in the mirror on the wall and remembered how nice I looked in my tan dress with white embroidered flowers. Lucia's was of the same material but a different design. They were special because our Zia Genovefa had made them for us, especially for this trip. I felt beautiful and cheered up. I began to dance around like I would on my grandfather's kitchen table.

"Let's explore and find the dining room." Mother took my hand and with Lucia in her arms, we began to explore passageways through the lower part of the ship. When we reached the deck with the dining rooms, my sister, still clutching the pocketknife, gingerly reached through a porthole and dropped the knife into the ocean. She screamed and demanded it back. Mother tried to calm her down. "I will get you another one." It wasn't the truth, but it allowed us to peacefully enter the dining room.

The three of us ate most of our meals in the spacious tourist-class dining room, one of the largest and most beautiful rooms I had ever seen. Tables with place settings for hundreds of people were arrayed with white tablecloths, white china, and vases of fresh flowers.

We searched for a table with room for us. We introduced ourselves to those at the table who would become our friends by the end of the voyage. We were familiar with most of the food, but not with the variety that was served. We never once went out to eat in Aielli; there were no restaurants.

We met our waiter, who would serve us all our meals for the length of the voyage. Tall and thin, with black hair and a smile, he greeted us: "Are you ready to order, Signora Campomizzi?" He offered us choices of rolls, pastries, and fruits, espresso for Mamma for breakfast, meatballs and pasta, roast beef, or leg of lamb for dinner. He would flip a slip of paper over his order book and bend down to meet my sister and me eye to eye.

"And Bambina Giovanna, and Bambina Lucia?"

Being addressed in such a formal way conferred importance, a big surprise for all of us. We felt like royalty. He would return with each course, shifting his way through a maze of tables and other waiters, balancing the weight of the huge serving trays with one hand above his shoulders, a living pendulum, over the sway of the ship beneath his feet. After dinner and before dessert, we chose from *mele*, *uva*, banana, *fichi*, and other fruits that I had never seen before. When we finished, our favorite waiter would reappear with dessert: delicious chocolate or strawberry gelato. Meals lasted a couple of hours with the adults talking and laughing over espresso while the children played simple games like hide and seek and danced around the floor.

After breakfast, when the weather allowed, we went for our daily walk on deck and visited with friends we had made during the voyage. We became close with several families.

One sunny late afternoon as we strolled the main deck before dinner, we met a couple with a six-year-old-daughter, Margarita. Margarita carried around in her arms a beautiful porcelain doll with soft blond curls and blue eyes. I was so excited about the voyage, about going to America, that I had not even thought about my doll until I saw Margarita's. I suddenly missed my doll deeply. We had left her behind. It broke my heart. For the first time since we left Aielli, I began to realize what it meant to leave behind the ones you love.

A day and a half after we left, the ship passed Gibraltar and glided through the Straits and out to the open ocean. With each passing wave, each mile, this ship was nearing America. Inside me, hope made anything possible or bearable. The anticipation in Mamma's smiles at the table when we ate, the music in her words as we ambled the decks, allowed the rhythm of the ocean to hypnotize our thoughts. Her eyes sparkled when out of nowhere she would begin to talk about Papa. Each day we were getting closer to him, to our new lives, to being together again.

During the fourth day of our trip, the ship hit turbulent waters, causing it to rock back and forth. We spent the next twenty-four hours cradled by our cabin, throwing up into our tiny sink, when we made it. The stewards checked up on us around meal times and brought us gelato, telling us to eat lightly. But by the next day, we were back to normal and returned to eating in the dining room.

One night after dinner, Margarita and her father came to our table to invite me to a movie in the ship's theater. Margarita and I were thrilled to be going to the theater together, even though I had no idea of what a movie was. I may have been impressed, but I fell asleep in the middle of it and had to be carried back to my cabin.

As the days passed, we were getting more anxious and more excited. The ship encountered fog. Unable to see anything, we sailed through the mist as if we weren't moving at all. Finally the announcement came: We were nearing New York Harbor.

When we finally spotted land, it was no more than a gray sliver on the western horizon. I stood on the big deck, watching, waiting, excited, and not knowing what to wonder. Wave by wave, the sliver thickened to a ribbon. Mile by mile, tall buildings began to inch their shadows into the sky. Other ships appeared on what I thought was an empty ocean. The coastline of my new world emerged.

In the distance, through cold January salt air, the Statue of Liberty rose above the harbor. At first no more than a blurry pencil point, she grew larger and larger as we slipped through the inlet between New York and New Jersey toward the Hudson River. Passing by her as a six-year-old, I only remember her as the biggest statue I had ever seen.

We landed at New York Harbor on the seventh day. Rain fell, and what was left of the fog shrouded Lady Liberty as we entered the harbor and tugboats came alongside to muscle our ship into its berth at Pier 84 at 44th Street. I couldn't wait to see my father and was jumping up and down with excitement. But we were but three of more than a thousand people assembling to go ashore, and there could be no rush in the discharge of so many passengers and so much cargo. It would take hours for the crew and dockworkers to lug all of the baggage from the ship.

We found Margarita's family and said our goodbyes.

"This has been the ride of a lifetime." Margarita's mother glanced up at the colors of the Italian flag crowning the stack of the *Andrea Doria*, then at the American flag on top of one of the import buildings, and smiled at my mother. "Can you believe it?"

I was still jumping up and down as I waved goodbye to Margarita and her doll.

On February 3, 1954, we stepped foot on American soil for the first time. The pier swarmed with passengers and workers and trucks and cabs, all strangers. Passengers arriving in New York Harbor had to wait for their belongings.

Two years later, in 1956, the MS *Stockholm* of the Swedish American Line hit the *Andrea Doria* and the Italian ship sank to the bottom of the Atlantic. As we stood beside the *Andrea Doria* on that day in February of 1954, I had no idea that ships that big could sink.

"Stay close to me." Mamma gripped my arm as if I would be swept away by the rush of people. She clenched Lucia with her other arm, straddling our suitcase as we began the long wait for the one trunk containing all our earthly possessions. I had never seen so many people in one place at one time. Mamma clutched her little brood, Lucia in her arms, suitcase at her feet, and I next to her, within an inch of her gray wool coat, awash in the flow of souls ebbing and flowing across the pier. I was most surprised by the people with dark skin. I had never seen a black person before, only people with black masks on Fat Tuesday, the big celebration of feasting before Lent begins.

"Is it Mardi Gras?" I tugged on my mother's coat. She didn't hear me. Her eyes scanned the waves of faces, looking not so much for a specific face, but for a face that recognized us.

Papa Domenico had seen to every detail of our journey, including making arrangements for relatives from Bayonne, New Jersey, to meet us. We waited, Mamma searching for our salvation, Lucia and I waiting for her. For a while, I thought about the beautiful forest green trunk trimmed in wood with brass hinges, somewhere in the hold of *Andrea Doria*, longing for the two small salamis Papa Domenico had smuggled into it. We waited for what seemed to be another two years to a six-year-old longing to be with her father again. Finally, two people rummaging through the crowd, sifting through masses of nameless faces with a handful of photographs, noticed us and stopped. They approached my mother, held up the photos like a couple of portrait artists, looked at Mamma, and looked at Lucia in her arms. One of them looked down at me and smiled. The other checked the photos in his hands.

"Are you Rodolfa, Giovanna, and Lucia?" he asked us in Italian, smiling.

Papa Domenico's relatives drove us to their small two-story house in Bayonne by way of a tunnel underneath the Hudson River. I was amazed that anyone could travel under so much water. We stayed at their home for the night. Their beds had no stones either. Very early the next morning, we boarded a train for Canton, Ohio, where my father would meet us at that station. Mamma told us that the people Papa lived with were bringing him to the station and taking us to our new home in Malvern.

CHAPTER 4

BARE FEET OF THE HEART

After a long train ride through the mountains of Pennsylvania into Eastern Ohio, I heard the call for the stop in Canton. Mamma and I peered through the windows of the train as it rumbled into Canton Station with its newest band of arrivals from New York's teeming shore. The cluster of souls wrapped up for the winter on the platform stirred as the train approached. I scanned the faces in the crowd, searching for the one I had waited two years to see.

"There . . . Mario!" Mamma cheered. She stood in the aisle of the train beside Lucy and me, bent over us, looking out the window. "There! You see Papa?"

I looked up at her, then followed her eyes and her grin. And there he was, leaning forward, seated on a bench with two older men and a woman. His dark eyes darted from coach to coach. Papa looked the same: tall and thin, just as I remembered, hard-shouldered from hard work. His short, dark, oiled hair glimmered in the late afternoon sun as the train belched to a halt. He spotted me in the window, stood up, crushed his cigarette under his heel, and ran through the crowd toward the train. I was the first off the train. Mamma and Lucia followed close behind. Papa grabbed Lucia in one arm, picked me up in the other by the waist of my fur-collared wool coat, and smiled as he said our names in a loud whisper.

"Giovanna! Lucia!"

Mamma stepped from the train like a star making an entrance. Dressed in a gray suit with a matching gray double-breasted coat, she dropped our suitcase on the platform, swaggered up to him, and wrapped her arms around him.

"Mario . . ."

They kissed and smiled, and my father set us down and stepped back. "Let me take a look at you." He beamed, but a trace of apprehension crossed his face.

We all piled into the car and Mr. Angeloni drove us to our new home in Malvern, just outside of Canton. It was a two-bedroom apartment above a two-car garage, with a wringer clothes washer in the back of the garage that the Angelonis rented. This was next door to a beer joint, or saloon, which they owned. Papa, with a cigarette in his mouth, sensed his wife's uneasiness and assured my mother that the stay was temporary.

Malvern, Ohio, became my home in the New World. We spent the first days after our arrival getting reacquainted with my father. He didn't look as tall as he had two years before. The thought never occurred to me that I was getting bigger.

Papa had furnished the apartment he rented from the Angelonis with a gray sofa and chairs. He had equipped the kitchen with a couple of iron skillets, pots and pans, mixing bowls, and a big pot and colander for pasta. Mamma was a good cook her entire life. She set to work establishing Aielli in our apartment over the garage. Mamma made her own pasta with a rolling pin. We eventually made our own sausage and bread, and sauce from fresh tomatoes. In the summer, we canned peaches as well as tomatoes, green beans, and other vegetables from Papa's garden. With eggs from a local farmer, we ate as well as we had in the Apennines.

Our landlords, Frank and Concentina, lived in an apartment next door behind their saloon. Often, Lucia and I would sit at one of the tables in the saloon before it opened. We spent time with their grandchildren, Edith and Frankie, eating potato chips, drinking soda, and learning English words.

A few days after I stepped foot on American soil, the Angelonis' daughter, Freda, and her daughter, Edith, stopped by our apartment and told my parents that they thought it would be a good idea for me to visit school with Edith the following Monday. Because of my November birthday, I could not begin school until the following September, but I could visit Mrs. Looby's first-grade classroom for a day. Edith spoke only English, so her mother translated. I knew very few English words, but I knew the meaning of the word *okay* when my parents agreed.

Early Monday morning, my mother made me two raw eggs beaten with sugar and a teaspoon of Marsala, the perpetual Italian breakfast, and helped me pick out my clothes. I wore one of the tan dresses and the pair of brown shoes that I wore on the *Andrea Doria*. Mamma brushed my hair and tied it at the top of my head with a big white bow. I ran down the stairs to the garage and out the door. Edith stood waiting in front of her grandparents' saloon. We stood on a little patch of blacktop next to the parking lot. We waited a few minutes, dancing with the cold, giggling and chatting over the language barrier. A big yellow bus stopped in front of Frank's saloon. A front wheel screeched as it halted, and did this at every stop all the way to school. I had never seen a school bus, much less ridden in one. Edith let me get on the bus first and I aimed straight for a window seat. The only time I had been out of our little home was the day before when we went to St. Francis Xavier Church in town for Mass in my father's car. We had neither cars nor buses in our village in Italy.

The ride would take about an hour each way, even after we moved into our own house down Route 43. I rode this bus all the way through eighth grade, zigzagging from crossroad to crossroad, farm to farm. The bus driver would gather students from first through twelfth grade to deposit them at the only two schools in town. As the numbers of riders rose, so did the jabbering, joking, and teasing. Like the uneven rhythm of the bounces the bus took when it passed over bumps in the road or railroad crossings, the driver barked orders for a quiet that never lasted. That first day, I didn't care. I was too excited to care about anything but going to school.

The school was in town, about a mile and a half down Route 43 to the west. The sun had just risen over the rolling hills of central Ohio. The scenery looked very different from my grandfather's grape vineyards, so different from the Apennine Mountains in Italy. It did not take long to learn that heavy trucks rumbled down the highway at all hours of the day and night on their way to towns and cities all over the Midwest. Rigs would growl their way back East with wheat and corn and canned goods and often bricks from the kiln my father worked at on the other side of Malvern.

The bus driver wheeled the bus into a parking lot next to a playground with swings, slides, and something called monkey bars. Edith and I jumped off the bus and skipped up the three steps through the door into the grammar school building.

My friend took my hand and walked me down the first-floor hallway of the three-story building to one of the first-grade classrooms. She smiled at me and pointed toward the woman standing in the doorway. "This is your room, Giovanna." Then

42

she scooted off to her third-grade classroom.

The teacher, wearing a plain tailored dark dress, knelt down to meet me face to face. I didn't understand what she said, but could tell she was happy to see me.

"I'm Mrs. Looby." Her eyes smiled beneath wavy dark hair streaked with gray, shorter it seemed to me than how women in Italy wore theirs. She put her hand on my shoulder. "Welcome to America, Giovanna, and to first grade." Mrs. Looby stood up, motioned me into the classroom, and pointed to a desk near the front of the room. "Please sit down."

I offered a bashful grin to the boys and girls already in the room as I walked to the desk and sat down. The desks were much smaller that the ones in my classroom in Italy but also had holes for inkwells. I looked around, smiled an unsteady smile as the room filled. Some of the thirty-five or so students looked at me. I was an oddity, a curiosity. I could feel my otherness, but I did not know what it meant. The girls' hair was longer, and some had braids; their dresses were longer and more colorful. The boys wore jeans or dress pants and shirts. My tan dress was short; matching tan laces graced my high-top brown leather shoes. My dark hair, cut into a bob, bore a large white bow. I was the only girl in the class with a bow in her hair. And I could not speak a word of English. A couple of girls stepped up to my desk trying to make me feel welcome. A blond-haired, blue-eyed girl about my size walked up from behind me, smiled, and set a first-grade reader down on the desk in front of me. I followed her finger as she opened the book to a page the class was currently working on, pointed to the picture, then to the word in the text below. I could understand nothing but their smiles.

"Boys and girls, I would like you to welcome Giovanna Campomizzi to our class," Mrs. Looby said. "Giovanna is new to our country and doesn't speak English, so please help her as best you can." Mrs. Looby stepped over to the blackboard. "Let's do some arithmetic." She chalked several addition and subtraction problems on the board and went to her desk to begin calling students up to solve the problems.

I was six years old. I don't know what came over me. All I knew was that though I could not speak English, I could speak arithmetic. I rose from my desk, walked over to the board, picked up a piece of chalk, solved each of the problems, went back to my desk, and sat down. As I sat down, I realized that I was smiling, very satisfied that I had just communicated in some way.

Students looked at me in silence. I think I was supposed to only solve one. Mrs. Looby eyed me from her desk with a questioning smile, rose, went to the blackboard and reviewed the problems with the class.

After math, Mrs. Looby announced recess. The students got up and stood next to their desks, then went to the cloakroom for their coats, hats, and mittens. They formed a straight line at the classroom door. I wondered what they were doing. She motioned for me to do the same. We went outside to play, and I learned the meaning of recess. I played with a couple of girls going down the slide, I learned how to use monkey bars, but the swings were the best. The wind blew in my face. I slipped into a daydream. I found myself alone with my thoughts about the days I played with my cousins outside my grandfather's house in Aielli.

I saw a pair of feet at the same time that I felt a pair of hands pull the swing to a stop. I looked up and realized that all the children were gone. A lady stood over me, telling me that recess was over. She took me by the hand and walked me back into school.

The boys and girls were copying spelling words from the board. Mrs. Looby reviewed them and went on to use them in sentences. I could see her point to a word and pronounce it. I tried to make the sounds, having no idea of what I was saying. I tried to look like I was following along, but I found myself utterly confused.

I knew lunchtime came when students started moving around. Mrs. Looby retrieved my lunch from the cloakroom and directed me to one of the tables at the side of the room where everyone ate. Even my food looked different: a salami sandwich on my mother's Italian bread, rather than thin-sliced bread from the grocery store, and a bag of chips Mamma bought from the Angelonis' saloon. Only my apple looked like what the other kids had.

After lunch, we worked at these tables for the rest of the day. Students took turns reading out loud from a picture book. I tried to make sense of the English words, but the effort made me very tired. I put my head down on the table and fell asleep until I felt a nudge that woke me up.

"Giovanna, it's time to go home." Mrs. Looby kept her hand on my shoulder. "Edith is at the door to help you get the right bus."

"*Grazie.*" I offered a shy wave to my classmates for a day.

We hopped on the bus and took the same seats we had that morning. Everyone was much noisier now that school was out. I was anxious to get home, to tell my mother and sister all about my day. Papa worked afternoons and nights. I would have to wait until the morning to tell him. It had been a long day, but I would have gladly returned the next day.

We were just beginning a new life in America. We had no toys but we didn't care. We played with the Angelonis' two grandchildren when they came home from school. Mamma cooked and sewed, just like she did in Italy. Snow fell in the winter, only in Ohio there was more of it. We visited my father's two sisters and their families, seven children among them. I don't remember learning English. I just absorbed the language during the months between our arrival in America in February and my first day of school in September.

One day in August 1954, about eleven in the morning just after the mail car arrived, Lucia and I escorted our mother to the mailbox.

"Let's get the mail, and after lunch visit the Angelonis." A small black-and-white butterfly circled the mailbox and continued circling, even as Mamma opened the cover and removed the mail.

"News from Papa Domenico." She ripped the flap from the envelope without opening it as we returned upstairs. Mamma made us lunch, usually leftover pasta or chicken soup from the night before, and sat down to read the news from home.

She took the letter from the envelope and read. Her hands began to tremble. She looked up, stared across the kitchen, then read the words again.

Cara Rodolfa,

I am saddened to tell you that your mother has died of a heart attack. Her weak heart that she suffered from all her life stopped working.

Maria brought up two cups of coffee for your mother and me. She placed them on our nightstands, her custom, and walked back downstairs. I was shaving in the bathroom.

"Domenico, your coffee is getting cold," your mother hollered to me. "Come here and drink it."

"I'm just going to finish shaving."

She was very quiet. When I returned to our room, she was lying on the bed, not moving. Maria went next door to get the doctor. There was nothing he could do. She did not suffer. I wish you were here. It is very difficult being so many miles away. I suffer your sorrow as well as my own.

Con amore,
Papa Domenico

We didn't go to the Angelonis'.

Mamma sent weekly letters to her family in Italy for years. There was a rural mailbox on a post outside the saloon next to Route 43, about twenty feet from the entrance to the tavern and the small door in the garage leading to the steps to our apartment. News from home was her lifeline to the only world she had known. She had given up her family for a promise, a promise to her husband, to be his for better or for worse. He had dreamed of being a teacher. Her dream of America was that of so many others who dreamt of coming to the United States, a land of prosperity where the streets were lined with gold and anything was possible. Now she found herself in America, in a

46

small apartment over a garage in a small town with two young daughters, her husband working nights earning just enough to keep them going. The letters from home were the hope that in time things would be in America as they had been in Italy. Each day, her trip to the mailbox became a ritual, like a silent prayer, unspoken, but the rite to the depths of her soul. As the years passed, so passed her memories of Italy, her youth, and her family, into those depths that none could feel or explain or understand but her.

My mother registered me for school in August. The day I officially began first grade, the Wednesday after Labor Day, was one of the happiest days of my life. I was elated and I had Mrs. Looby for my first teacher.

Mrs. Looby kept a violin next to her desk and made it a daily routine to play a short piece of patriotic music to start the day. Our first duty of the day was to stand and recite the Pledge of Allegiance and a short prayer. I knew the words to neither. By the time I arrived at first grade, I could speak, but not read, English. What I heard from my teachers and my classmates, I was able to understand and remember.

Before class began, Mrs. Looby took attendance. She called out the names of each person in the classroom, and when she came to me, I heard the Americanized version of my name for the first time: Joann Campomizzi. I almost jumped out of my seat. The Angelonis had told Lucia and me that our names would change to sound more American, be more American — that I would become Joann and she Lucy. When I heard my name called, I smiled, sat up tall in my seat, and felt as much a part of America as anyone in the State of Ohio.

One day, about three weeks after school began, we all settled into Papa's Chevrolet and made a trip into town. Papa pulled along the curb in front of the local five-and-dime. Mamma reached over the front seat and handed me a dollar bill.

"Run in and get a box of envelopes for me," she said in Italian.

I knew why she asked me and felt a surge of pride as I walked into the store. I smiled at the clerk and asked her for bags. I didn't know the word for envelopes.

"No," I said when the clerk handed me a large brown bag. "The kind you put letters in."

"Oh," she turned and grabbed a banded stack of envelopes from the shelf behind her. "You mean these."

I barely smiled as I left the store, but I felt a rush of triumph as my mother rolled down her window. I handed her the envelopes and her change. It was the beginning of my career as my mother's translator and spokesperson. I knew so little about my new country, but I felt confident.

By the beginning of October, another American tradition made its way to Malvern. Papa and I were visiting the parents of a boy my age named Tommy. They lived on Route 43, about a mile from his grandparents' saloon.

"Are you dressing up for Halloween?" Tommy scoffed. "I'm going to win first prize for the best costume, but you can enter if you want to."

I stuck out my tongue. "You can't talk to me like that."

The garage we were playing in was filled with toys. Tommy's family was well-to-do. As hard as I tried to be his friend, he was not my friend. He made fun of me because I didn't speak English very well and mocked my clothes and shoes.

He continued his teasing. "When you get home, ask your mother if she has a Halloween costume for you. I bet she doesn't."

I suddenly felt very small, about the size of one of his toys.

When Papa and I got home, I found my mother at the kitchen sink, daydreaming as she washed the dishes.

"The town is having a Halloween parade. Can I be in it?"

She looked at me a bit surprised. Halloween was not a celebration for children in Italy. For us, it was the eve of All Saints' Day, a more solemn event. For me it was one day away from my birthday.

"I need a costume," I said, knowing she wouldn't let me down.

Mamma became caught up in my excitement. She looked out of the window over the sink for a minute. "I will make you a fine costume . . . a gypsy dress."

She dried her hands and left the kitchen for what seemed like a month. I chatted with Lucy, who was sitting at the kitchen table with a plate of *pizzelles*. Sounds from drawers and the closet in the bedroom echoed through the apartment. My mother returned, smiling as if she had just won a week's worth of groceries, and laid the remnants of six pieces of gauze and brightly colored chiffons on the table, each different.

She arranged patterns and colors on the table to make the bodice, sleeves, and skirt of the dress. Usually when my mother made me a dress, she pinned all of the pattern pieces on the fabric and cut the fabric to match the pieces. This time she used no pattern, nor cut any fabric. Instead, she fit the dress on me, pinning the front and back bodices together and adding the sleeves — one with a small blue print, the other, red with a large print. She gathered the yellow, pink, and green prints together for the skirt as I stood next to the table, restless and excited. She finished the pinning, stepped back with a gleam in her eyes, tossed a handful of pins on the table, surveyed her creation, and gave me a smile.

My dress looked authentic. I remember seeing gypsies in Naples before leaving Italy. My relatives told me to watch out for them, that they were not good people, but I loved how they dressed so brightly. And now I was going to be one of them for Halloween.

I knew she would make something beautiful, and she had. I felt beautiful. I danced around the kitchen until Mamma made me take the dress off.

Through the week, my mother basted together the pieces of fabric, using loose stitches for the seams so the dress could be easily taken apart. She finished it two days before the parade. I knew she fit, rather than cut, the materials for a reason. She had purchased the fabric to send as a gift to Zia Genovefa to make dresses for my two cousins, Erminia and Elisa. No cloth was ever wasted. Mamma had me try my costume on now and then to adjust the fit, but she refused to let me wear it until Halloween. I think she was afraid the stitching would not take a lot of strain.

One afternoon, as we were fitting my outfit, the sound of footsteps scuffed the stairs, followed by a knock on the apartment door.

"Hi, Mrs. Campomizzi, can Joann come out and play?" Tommy asked.

My mother smiled and waved him in. Tommy entered the kitchen behind her, eyeing my costume with a smirk on his face. Mamma returned to her work, pinning a piece of soft blue gauze around my waist. "Don't move, Giovanna. I need to find one more piece of chiffon." She left for the bedroom.

"That isn't for Halloween," Tommy whispered with a grin. "Get yourself a real costume."

The words hit like a punch. I forced myself not to cry.

"Just wait. You'll see what a Halloween costume actually looks like." And he was out the door as quickly as he had arrived. He succeeded in dashing my good mood.

Mamma banked around the corner into the kitchen with the blue remnant draped over her arm and stopped in her tracks when she saw the tears welling up in my eyes. One of the kitchen chairs stood in the middle of the room for me to stand on when Mamma needed me higher for measurements near the bottom of my costume. She sat down on a chair a couple of feet away and looked at me. We were now eye to eye, not adult to child, but human being to human being. I looked into her eyes until I could no longer contain the hurt, then wrapped my arms around her and cried.

"Don't pay any attention to Tommy, he is acting like he always does: a spoiled brat."

On the day of the parade, my mother dressed me in my costume. Papa, Mamma, Lucy, and I drove the two miles into town. I was six years old and wanted to win this competition and prove to Tommy that I was as good as he was.

Just before the parade, Tommy came and stood next to me, wearing a white cowboy hat and holding a guitar.

"Now *this* is a Halloween costume," he taunted.

The Malvern High School Marching Band began to play as our menagerie of fantasy rambled down Main Street toward the improvised grandstand at Main and First where town officials would judge us. I marched next to Susan, one of my newfound friends, who was always the best dressed girl at school. Her costume transformed her into an ugly witch for the competition. For an afternoon, we were who we pretended to be. Betty dressed like Cinderella, Jimmy like Abe Lincoln, Luke like Superman. We gathered in front of the grandstand where the mayor called each child up on the stage, from youngest to oldest, to be judged by him and four officials.

"You don't deserve to win a prize." Tommy said, yanking on my dress before our names were called. The panels Mamma had stitched began to separate. I held them together as I pushed his hand away. I wanted to cry. I didn't know what to do.

I hoped with all my heart that he didn't win a prize. He had pushed me around so much and been so mean. I yearned to be back in Italy with my cousins where I knew I would be accepted. Anger can boil in a six-year-old. I wanted to beat him up, but more than that, I wanted to be good and accepted in this community.

About forty-five grade-school children fidgeted on the stage, waiting for the winner to be announced. I stood wedged in the middle of the muted crowd; Tommy made sure that he was front and center.

Mamma knew her trade. The panels of my dress held as I made my way up to the stage. The judges inspected and discussed, reviewed and huddled, pondered and weighed. As was the custom, third and second place were announced first.

"And first place . . . Joann Campomizzi."

I felt a shock so intense that it snatched a breath from me. My classmates made way for me. Tommy, in the center of the front row, had to step aside to let me pass. In the middle of the crowd stood my parents.

Mamma beamed, clapping her hands in the air as she spun around like a gypsy. She was as happy as a lark. My father's broad grin glowed over the crowd. I had waited two years to see him again and here, for the first time in America, I could offer him a sense of pride in something I—and my mother—had accomplished.

Tommy continued the badgering, but now I felt a confidence that softened the blows. He taught me that life in America was not everything I had imagined. There would be highs as well as lows. Roses have thorns. But on Halloween of 1954, I could see only roses, and America was glorious.

CHAPTER 5

MY ANGEL IN HEAVEN

Our new sister, Erminia, was born on Saturday, February 5, 1955, at Mercy Hospital in Canton, Ohio, the nearest hospital to Malvern. My parents took great pride in the fact that she came into the world as an American citizen. As my mother was making breakfast, she stopped and calmly told my father that it was time to go to the hospital. Lucy and I were left with the Angelonis. Papa came home late that night to tell us we had a new baby sister with a round, chubby face, dark brown hair, and dark blue-gray eyes. Five days later, Mother arrived home with Erminia, unwrapped her from a white blanket and bunting, and lay her on our gray sofa. We didn't have a bassinet, only a crib in the bedroom, so the sofa became Erminia's post during the day.

Papa still worked nights. Lucy was not yet in school, a four-year-old forever on the move. I came home from school each day and willingly tended to Mom while she nursed Erminia. I played with my new sister at her perch on the sofa when Mother was busy taking care of the rest of us.

On the weekends, Papa and I could take turns. He would bring his coffee to the living room, sit next to Erminia, smile, try to have her make facial gestures, encourage her to coo and smile back, to react as babies do.

I don't remember her being ill. But since Papa's time at home was more sporadic than for the rest of us, as the months passed, I think he was the first to notice that something wasn't right. Erminia turned her head from side to side and looked around the room, but I never heard her laugh. And she didn't cry, she whimpered. As time went on and her eyes ripened to a beautiful walnut brown, they would gaze off into the middle of the living room at nothing at all. The morning my parents finally called our doctor to the house, Erminia was thirteen months old and had not yet learned to crawl or walk.

I didn't go to school that day. Mother usually woke and dressed the baby for the day, but that morning Erminia was running a fever and was very lethargic. We were all in the bedroom when Dr. Stires arrived. He gave our little sister a shot and told my mother to apply cold compresses to cool her down and to call him if anything changed. Through the day, I could tell by the worried look on my mother's face that Erminia was getting worse rather than better. She made the call she didn't want to make. When Dr. Stires returned, Mother put her arms around Lucy and me.

"Pray," she said, then sent us out of the bedroom.

We went and stood in front of wood-framed statues of Jesus and Mary hanging on the varnished wooden living room wall.

"Please, God, don't let our sister die." We prayed and prayed, hoping that if we prayed long and hard enough, she would live. Occasionally, the murmur of the doctor's soft-spoken voice in the bedroom sifted through our pleas. Afternoon descended into evening. We prayed. We waited. We fidgeted. We prayed more.

The sound of Mother's steps coming down the hall broke the spell. We turned and moved toward her. Her face showed only a blank stare of resignation. We put our arms around her as she put hers around us.

"Erminia is in heaven with Jesus and Mary."

Some time later, the funeral director, Mr. Deckman, carried my sister out of the house, her body placed in a small white wicker basket with two handles.

We held the wake in our living room. Mr. Deckman covered one wall with a white satin cloth. I will always remember that wall by Erminia's casket. Many townspeople came to pay their respects, as did my father's family: Uncle Ettore, Aunt Emma, Papa Giovanni, and Mamma Victoria, who by now also lived in Malvern, along with my Uncle Vince, Uncle Charlie, and Aunt Lucy. I could not believe my eyes when I saw Mrs. Beach, my second-grade teacher, come through the front door of our house to console our family. I was despondent, but I felt honored she had come.

By the night of the funeral, my father, Uncle Vince, and Papa Giovanni had been drinking most of the day. The men were in the kitchen; we were in the living room. These were the only rooms we had besides two bedrooms and a bathroom. They recalled stories, laughed to spite the pain, and carried on until they grew tired and everyone finally went home, leaving our home and its occupants to the barren silence of loss.

People were trying to deal with their sadness. Alcohol became my father's refuge—and religion my mother's. For weeks after my sister's death, I could see my mother standing silently before the statues of Jesus and Mary for long periods of time. She began carrying her rosary beads everywhere she went, whispering the prayers through her daily chores. In time, the wound began to heal. Mother seemed to come to terms with death, accepting its embrace as an inevitable part of life, finding a deeper joy in taking care of Lucy and me. Her rosary would become her constant companion, along with her Italian prayer book, now torn, taped, dog-eared, coverless, but to her, irreplaceable.

When my baby sister was born, we had not lived in Malvern very long. We knew very few people. We had been in the United States only two years when she died. Mother knew one person fairly well: Lucy, the lady who picked up and delivered clothing for the local dry cleaner. Mamma had asked if she and her husband would consider being godparents for Erminia. Lucy readily agreed. After Erminia's death a year later, while Mother spent months trying to cope with the loss, Lucy and her husband, Scottie, would stop by to talk or drop off some food, just to show that they were thinking of us.

Christmas of that year, Lucy and Mary, a friend of hers, came to our house with a small pine tree, lights, and decorations, and set up our very first tree in our living room. The two placed gifts they had wrapped under the tree. They also presented us with cookies. They quite literally created the holiday for us. We were poor but proud. We had nothing to give in return but, for the sake of my sister Lucy and me, my parents accepted the gesture. It was one of the best Christmases ever. Mother never forgot their kindness. She, Lucy, and Mary remained friends their entire lives.

CHAPTER 6

PAPA DOMENICO'S VISIT

Gradually life returned to its small-town rural routine.

It must have been fall or winter of the year my sister died — we were all wearing coats — when our third-grade class walked across the parking lot of Malvern Local School to the auditorium of the high school to hear a performance by a group of gospel singers. Arranged by height with the rest of the entire student body, we settled into seats near the stage, only feet from where the group would sing.

When the troupe of smiling black women filed out onto the stage, I had no idea of what they would be singing. I had never heard gospel music before. I thought of my last day on the *Andrea Doria* when we arrived in New York City and I saw black people for the first time. Now I was beginning to feel like a real American. I was fluent in English, and if I thought about the color of someone's skin, it was no more surprising than noticing the color of a flower.

They sang. They clapped their hands. And they encouraged everyone in the auditorium to sing along with them and clap their hands. Their voices were beautiful, their harmonies and rhythms hypnotizing. One song, "He's Got the Whole World in His Hands," I still remember. An audience of hundreds of students, from first graders to high school seniors, sang and clapped to the lead of the women onstage, kneading the passion of their devotion into one soul and one voice. It was a wonderful day.

On a bright June day in 1957, our landlords, Frank and Concentina Angeloni, drove my family and me to the Canton Train Station for the first time since our arrival in 1954. This time Papa Domenico would be getting off the train. I was nine years old and still remembered and revered him. I had not seen my grandfather for three years, but when he stepped off the train, I recognized him immediately. Erect, with a military bearing that never left him and with quick, deliberate steps, he strode across the platform with a smile that felt like he had been carrying it all the way from Italy. He bent over and wrapped Lucy and me in hugs and kisses.

"*Bambine*! I spotted you a mile away!" My grandfather spoke English and Italian.

Papa Domenico stood up and hugged Mamma as he gave her a kiss on the cheek. He stepped back, grasped her shoulders, and looked her in the eyes with those pale blue eyes of his that had dimmed a bit.

"Rodolfa, you don't look well. Are you taking care of yourself?"

"Papa, you worry too much. We're just very busy." She grabbed his hand and led us all to the car. "Welcome." Perhaps she didn't recognize how sad she had been.

Papa Domenico greeted Dad and the Angelonis with the courtesy of old acquaintances. Dad had been born in Flushing, about an hour away, but had moved to Malvern because families from Aielli had settled there.

"Enough of this." He grabbed his suitcase from a passing baggage cart. "We can talk in the car. How long to Malvern?"

I loved having my grandfather visit because he paid a lot of attention to me. He would read through my reader and geography books with me. He praised me and told me how smart I was. When I came home from school, he would look through my papers and ask me what I had done that day. Before supper, I would read to him. I can still see him sitting on a red kitchen chair, rarely uttering a word, and leaning in, listening as I read. He encouraged and praised more than he corrected, and I was so proud to show him that I had learned to read and write in English.

The Christmas season was much, much happier with him in the midst of our family. I read the story of the first Christmas, and my mother made date pinwheels, bow ties, crème-filled cookies, fig-stuffed cookies, and *pizelles*. I helped in the kitchen when I could. I wanted to show my grandfather that I was growing into someone he could be proud of. Lucy and I each received a medal of the Blessed Virgin on a gold chain and, of course, a bag of Hershey's Kisses.

Mom wanted to buy Papa Domenico a present, although she couldn't afford it. She put a winter jacket for him on layaway at

Rice's Department Store and started making payments on it starting in September.

On the eve of the Nativity, Mom, Dad, Papa Domenico, Lucy, and I attended Midnight Mass at St. Francis Xavier Catholic Church in Malvern. Our custom was to go home and celebrate, eating the cookies Mom had made. The next day we feasted on our best meal since coming to America, compliments of my grandfather's chivalry. He loved his coat, and it fit perfectly. Mom said he later gave her back the money that she had used to buy it.

Papa Domenico stayed in the States for almost a year but did not spend the entire time with us. He went to Washington, DC, for some meetings. He also visited family and friends in southern Ohio and Bayonne, New Jersey. During the more temperate seasons, he would journey off to parts far and near to meet friends who had survived the war or to spend some time with family, friends, or acquaintances who had moved to the US from Italy. He had honor down to the marrow, and love for life.

Three years after his wife's death, he had left six daughters to tend to the rustic family home in Aielli and set off to take another look at the world. The first purpose for his visit was to spend time with his daughter and her family. Loyalty brought him to the home of his one daughter who had left Italy for America. Though not entirely convinced of her happiness, he, as he had done in Aielli years before, accepted her decision to be where she was.

He left with a bit of reluctance the day we drove him to the train station in Canton, but leave he did — for Bayonne and New York City and a ship back to Italy.

Who was I going to read to? Who was going to reward us with chocolate kisses? I grew lonely. I turned to school and buried myself in my work. This helped my spirit.

At school, I received very good grades and earned the respect of my teachers. My English was as good as anyone's in the class, but I could not avoid feeling different. Mother was an excellent seamstress, but being from a small farming town in the mountains of Italy, she had little formal education. Father was an educated man, but the chronic physical pain he lived with and the emotional wreckage of war had stripped him of the ability to concentrate for very long. As part of an immigrant family, my clothes were different, the food I brought for lunch was different, and our family customs were different. I rarely had a birthday party because we did not celebrate them. Holidays were events of significance more religious than social. I wanted to be part of the social fabric around me, but I did not want to be led by the herd. I wanted to be accepted, but I did not want to forsake myself in order to do so.

One Saturday in October, when I was in fifth grade, my father's friend Bob called me out to the kitchen. He used to routinely drop in on Saturdays to have a beer with Dad. They both worked at the local brick plant and shared rides. Bob handed me two ladies' dress catalogs.

"Joann, I'm going to buy you a dress. Look through these and pick out something you like."

I wish to this day that I could have seen the look on my face. I was utterly bewildered. I had never had a store-bought dress in my life. Mother made all of our clothes. I swooned over pictures of dresses for two weeks. I could not decide. I wanted to jump out of my skin.

Two Saturdays later, Bob made his usual stop to visit Dad. This time he led me to Rice's, the one and only department store in town. Mrs. Gidley, a neighbor, worked there and greeted us with a smile. It was clear from the way the two of them spoke that Bob had stopped in to the store beforehand. I tried on several dresses and finally picked one out, a red and dark-green plaid dress, brass-buttoned in the front and gathered at the waist. I wore that dress, store-bought and special, once a week for a year.

Mrs. Bell, my fifth-grade teacher and a clotheshorse herself, said to me, "Joann, I just adore your new dress." She noticed that a boy in my class, whom she always referred to as ST, had caught my attention. She let me know with a snicker or a smile that the dress would do the trick. Clothes became another way of belonging, a means of coping.

CHAPTER 7

THE RECORD PLAYER

One holiday that did change for us as we adjusted to the customs of our new world was Christmas. In Italy we received a small gift, not on *Natale* (Italian for Christmas), the holy day itself, but on the Feast of Epiphany on January 6 to celebrate the visit of the Three Wise Men to the baby Jesus with gifts of gold, frankincense, and myrrh. The night before Christmas, as folklore has it, La Befana, a kindly old woman who helped the wise men find the Holy Child, flies on her magic broom from house to house leaving a little present—a small paper bag filled with fruit and nuts—for good children in their homes. In America we gradually adopted the celebration of Christmas, but gifts beyond fruit and nuts were rare at first.

So it happened during these days that a burning desire for a record player that played 45 rpm records seized my idle thoughts, my daydreams, pauses in between chews at supper, moments waiting for someone to find me among cornstalks in the fields as we played hide and seek, long stretches waiting for water to boil for pasta when I helped with supper. I wanted a record player. From summer on, whenever I could, however I could work this dream into any conversation with my mother, I dropped hints. I do not remember her ever paying any particular attention to my pleas.

At this time, Mom worked part time cleaning the office of our family doctor. Each year at Christmastime, Dr. Stires would present Mom with fifty dollars, which she used to buy our gifts and extras for our dinner: ham and ground beef for the tiny meatballs in her lasagna, ingredients for a rum cake, and of course fruit and nuts for our stockings. Since Cumara Lucy, Erminia's godmother, and her friend Mary had brought us our first little tree the year Erminia died, we adopted the custom of placing a tree in our living room—sparsely decorated and with a cement block for a stand, but still our very own Christmas tree.

This particular year, we attended Midnight Mass, as was our custom, and returned home for custard-filled Christmas cookies. There, beneath the tree, was a record player.

It came with one 45 of instrumental music. Mom had used part of her bonus to buy it for me and a pair of ice skates for my sister Lucy.

I don't know how many times I played that one record. That record player brought me to my imagination, a place where I could dream, I could imagine, I could escape.

During this time, Dad worked evenings at the brick plant in Minerva, another small town in the area. We did not see much of him during the week. In one sense, our life was typical of the generation: Dad was the breadwinner, Mom the homemaker. Each summer, Dad grew and tended a huge vegetable garden alongside the house. We had bought our own house several years after our arrival. In season, Mom and I would harvest green beans, cucumbers, zucchini, peppers, onions, tomatoes, and lots of potatoes. During the growing season we never bought produce — we canned enough to last us through winter.

However, my father's greatest daily battle was his affection for a bottle of beer. Dad used to frequent the local beer joints, as bars were called in the 1950s. He was easy to get along with because he was very happy-go-lucky, especially when he was smoking a cigarette and drinking a beer. I should say he *appeared* happy, because this wasn't always the case.

He worked very hard as a laborer in a clay pit five days a week but knew how to have a good time when he was home or with his friends. Dad had spent two years on his own, either cooking his own food or eating at the Angelonis', but whenever he ate, he liked a beer with his meals. Occasionally, after we finished supper on a Saturday night, Dad would throw a coat on his back, pull the cigarette from his mouth, lean over the back of my mother's chair, and smile into her face. "Do you want to go for a ride?"

The Corner Café was a pleasant place, and the handful of patrons seemed to treat it as a second living room. Mother tolerated the pleasantry, but after an hour or so, she grew impatient for home. Occasionally Papa would take us to a different bar, but in rural Ohio the taverns were working-class places with working-class patrons and all pretty much the same. All that Lucy and I knew was that it was a night out and sometimes we could go inside and have fun playing the shuffle bowling machines.

About ten tables surrounded a dance floor where a couple or two would dance to music that spilled from a jukebox next to the long wooden bar, worn bare in places by elbows and glasses. We would sit at one of the tables, nibbling our treats and listening to the music while Papa chatted and joked around with his friends at the bar. He routinely stopped by our table to check on how we were doing.

"Are you having a good time?" He knew that Lucy and I were enjoying our night out. Papa wanted Mamma to have a good time, knowing that she was keeping track of the hours. She would cross her arms and smile. Dad would sit with us long enough to sip a beer and have another cigarette, then he slipped back to the bar.

Looking back, our hope was to rise through the ranks of American prosperity, but in those days of hard work, little money, and even fewer frills, we somehow eked out a contentment — an afterthought almost — that I could only describe as happiness.

There were many days that my dad was kind and gentle. During the course of the year that my grandfather lived with us, my father controlled his outbursts. Whether this was due to the strength of Papa Domenico's spirit, I cannot say. All I know for certain is that the tension in our lives eased somewhat.

The rest of the time in Malvern, Father spent many a day yelling and scaring Lucy and me. In hindsight, he suffered. His wounds from the war left scars and pain. Today we would say that he probably suffered from post-traumatic stress disorder (PTSD).

Saturday mornings were mostly pleasant and he told us stories. I feared him on some of the other days. As a young girl, I didn't understand. At times I spoke back to him. It was not a good idea.

CHAPTER 8

MY FATHER'S WATER

The first place my father went to each morning was the refrigerator for a plastic pitcher, the kind that never wears out but turns yellow with age. It sat in the refrigerator holding Dad's water.

He always spat in his water so we would not touch it. Early one typical Saturday morning when I was around eleven, I poured my father a cup of coffee. He had rolled some cigarettes the night before. The hand-rolled cigarette barely held together in his hand as he took a puff, smoking in between slurps of coffee with four heaping tablespoons of sugar to make it almost like syrup, sickeningly sweet. When he opened the refrigerator door, he hadn't seen his pitcher. Not typical. He glared at my sister and me as we cowered in our pajamas over our raw eggs and Marsala. Mother buttered bread in silence in the corner of the kitchen.

"Where's my water?" He locked up like a statue.

"We didn't touch it!" I cried. Lucy huddled next to me in silence. She would not dare to answer him back or move his pitcher.

Father rummaged through the only shelf tall enough to hold the pitcher and eventually found it. We knew the rules. We didn't touch his water. We did not touch his drinking glasses, which had their own special place in the cupboard. This was because we drank milk. My father did not. If anyone put milk in his pitcher or one of his glasses, he would fly into a rage.

He had poured himself a glass of water and sat down to his coffee at one end of the table. Mother poured herself a cup of coffee and sat down in silence opposite us. Lucy swirled the egg in her glass, trying to make designs with the yolk, drank it down, and shuffled over and sat on Mother's lap.

I couldn't understand Dad's behavior. There were days when he behaved as normally as any father I could imagine, laughing and joking around with us. Days when the contentment and security of family life were not even a conscious thought. Then days like this would come along when my father's past eclipsed any rational judgment, leaving him and us to the furies of memories he could not vanquish or explain. He looked at us, through us, as if he had nothing to say and everything to say. Papa leaned on the table with his left arm, his hand and its two crippled fingers clearly visible.

"You see these broken parts of me all the time," he said, with a trace of remorse in his voice and a thinly veiled terror in his eyes. "I've told you a little about what the German camps were like. Some of the Germans made people suffer. They hated people who weren't German. The simplest thing to say is that camps were very bad places. I know it's hard to believe, but I did this to myself," he said, glancing at his fingers. "I was scarred. I hit my foot with a sledgehammer because then you would go to the camp hospital. You would get some soup." He lifted his left pant leg, revealing its calf half the girth of his right, with a long scar down the shin. "I hurt my leg. The scars are all here."

I still did not know why he hated milk. This was not a dislike, but an utter loathing. I could not understand it; milk, the first food that babies take from their mother's breasts, sweet and good. All that any of us knew was that he had suffered something terrible. We knew he was afraid. He always slept with the bedroom light on. We knew his screams in the middle of the night, the terror in his eyes the morning he woke up yelling at some invisible enemy, moments when the past sucked him back into a present that he could not escape, the times he would drink a couple of beers and just lay his head in his arms and go stone silent for a very long time. Only rarely did he ever mention details in a rational state of mind, as if he were certain that reason held no power over hell, and to even mention it would drag him into an insanity that would keep him there forever.

"The Germans killed people by the millions." Father stared into the table, a handsome thirty-five-year-old, stone still, shuddering through his eyes from a terror within. "They built furnaces to burn the dead . . . it's true . . . they stacked the dead like firewood along the walls, in heaps as more and more prisoners were crammed into the camp . . . more and more executions . . . more and more trains from other camps with as many dead as living on them.

"Me and others finally got out of there. Thanks to the Americans. Two other guys and I started making our way south, travelling by night and hiding during the day, in barns when we could find them. We knew only too well what the Germans were capable of and were terrified of them."

Father crushed out his cigarette and held his glass of water with both hands. "Cows . . . we could get milk. It's six hundred miles from Munich to home. We hid, we ran, we lived on milk, convincing ourselves that if we ran hard enough and far enough we could break free from what we had lived through—but there was no running from that hole from hell." He lit another cigarette. "I never want to see another drop of milk for as long as I live."

As a little girl in Aielli, one night I felt a pair of arms grab me from my bed and ferry me downstairs where everyone was huddled in terror. An earthquake had trembled our little town. There was no place to run when the very ground began rumbling beneath the villagers' feet. Even as a little girl I could feel the fear of the adults who rarely showed such an emotion. They did the only thing they could do: wait, and pray that the scourge would pass.

My father was solid and strong. I loved him, but I feared him in his dark moods, when these earthquakes trembled within him. I longed for the ground to stop shaking.

Mother looked into his eyes, reached over, and laid her hand across his wrist. "You're their father," she said to him.

Lucy slipped from Mamma's lap and stole off to our bedroom. I helped Mother clear the table and left Father to his water and his silence.

CHAPTER 9

THE AGONY AND THE ECSTASY

My dad rarely discussed what his life was like before he was taken into the Italian army, only that he wanted to be a teacher. Dad left Aielli in the 1930s to attend university in L'Aquila, a small city about a half hour north of us. He studied to become a teacher and planned to marry Mother when he finished his studies. However, World War II consumed Europe, and in 1942 Mussolini scraped universities for soldiers. Italy drafted Papa and hauled him off to war. He trained as a telegraph operator and served until captured by the Germans after the Allied invasion of southern Italy. They shipped him around as a prisoner until his arrival at Dachau. Mother was in limbo.

My father's brother, Uncle Vince, came to America when I was seven years old. We spent a lot of time together until he married and moved from Malvern. Over the years, we really liked talking with each other, and he would tell me about Mom and Dad.

"Your parents were married on February 18, 1946, less than a year after your father's return to Aielli. Your mother had promised to wait for him and kept her promise, although she was very beautiful and pursued by other young men. Like every soldier coming home, your father wanted to return to a normal life.

"Your mother was the fourth of nine girls. She carried her share of cooking and cleaning, working the fields, and harvesting in the olive groves."

Nearly three years without news of Mario, however, had left an imprint on her soul. Mom worked, but she worked more silently, with less liveliness, as the war lugged life into deeper and deeper uncertainty. Just one more of millions in a decimated Europe, wondering if a reason for living still existed. But duty existed even at home. She wanted to be a good and faithful servant, though no one seemed to pay any particular attention.

Word had spread that the war was over. Italy was in shambles. The country had been overrun by two invading armies, its cities had been bombed, many of its roads and bridges had been destroyed, soldiers and civilians alike wandered the countryside trying to regain some sense of what *the war is over* really meant. The little village of Aielli had escaped most of the destruction, and life in the fields went on in spite of the ravaging of Italy.

One afternoon, as Mamma walked with a basket of figs on her head that she had picked from one of the fig trees scattered through a nearby olive grove, a neighbor passing by told her that Mario had come home. She stared at him in disbelief. The big-bellied, heavy man told her that three ragged men had come through a vineyard from the north. One bony-looking form of a man headed into town as the other two moved on toward the south.

Mario!

Terrified that Mario might catch sight of her in a dirty dress walking around with a basket of figs on her head, she ran across a field in the opposite direction toward home. They had grown up together since his arrival from America when he was four years old. Their homes were no more than a few minutes' walk from each other. University stretched the distance between them and deepened their affection. Germany had nearly destroyed it.

"Your father went to school to become a teacher," Mother said many times over the years, very proud of his intentions. "He was very smart, but the war ruined him. It changed his life forever."

An emaciated figure clothed in rags had returned, with a weathered beard and shocks of brown hair on his head. At least sixty pounds lighter than the last time she had seen him, my father looked as though his skin draped nothing but bones.

Mario and Rodolfa married about six or seven months after his return to Aielli. This must have given him time to fill out and fit back into his clothes. At first, his mother made him walk around town for a week in the rags he had arrived in, unwilling to buy him clothes that fit. This incensed my mother and she never forgot it.

CHAPTER 10

THE EYE OF THE BEHOLDER

As I grew, so did my determination — stubbornness, if you will. This trait emerged as boldness, a confidence that served to mask anger and fear I knew but refused to own. In school, I focused intently on achieving good grades as a means to overcome the fear that I was fundamentally of less value than my classmates and friends.

My sixth-grade class held court in the high school due to a lack of room in the elementary school building. I loved being in the high school. I could watch all of the upper-class boys in the halls and the cafeteria. They teased my friends and me. The arrangement delighted me.

The reigning monarch of this era was Mr. Becknell, a tall, thin, middle-aged teacher with a neatly trimmed mustache and short-cropped dark red hair. His beady, penetrating blue eyes gave me the creeps and he stared me down if I challenged him. He struck me as odd, always dressed in the European style of the day for men: a sweater or suit coat and matching tie over a white dress shirt. His imperial height gave him an air of authority, and I was a little awed by his grasp of worldly affairs. His intelligence was capacious and, at times, condescending. He spoke disparagingly of Catholics and often ridiculed students who failed to think answers through. But he was a great storyteller and often related tales about his experiences in Africa during World War II.

"There were two very clever men who wandered the Allied encampments in North Africa during the war. One would sell a large red and green plaid wool blanket, clearly obtained from a British unit somewhere, and a clear and present catch for a bloke during cold desert nights. The other would come along and play policeman, claiming that the blanket was stolen, and nick it back from the soldier who had just bought it. They did this over and over and made lots of money."

I shot my hand up. "This is very dishonest and wrong," said I in my righteous indignation. His routine response to my moral outrage was to place his hand under his chin, as if he were pondering my position, say nothing, and move on to the next topic. My need to be right often brought us to this crossroad. I had been taught the American ideal of equality for all. I had also experienced the prejudice and injustice of American reality. There were times when I had no idea what his eyes were saying. In those days, spanking was still allowed in school. I witnessed a few of the boys getting paddled, and I thought I might be punished. More than once, when I questioned him, I hid in the girls' bathroom during recess until I could join the rest of the students back in the classroom. But ultimately all I had to endure was a spell of Mr. Becknell's silent treatment. I think he tolerated my insolence because he knew by what I said that I was listening to him. He may not have liked some of it, but he respected honesty.

Not only did I want to succeed, I needed to succeed. I loved school. I loved learning. Education did not care if you were born in another country. It was free for the taking.

I shared classrooms with some of the very smart students— intimidating, especially when it came to exams, but I loved the competition. The Ohio Achievement Test is a statewide test to measure what students have learned and are capable of in a variety of subjects. We were given this test in eighth grade. Miss Ayers—a tall, thin, middle-aged schoolmarm, and a wonderful teacher—came to class one day with a large brown cardboard box full of papers. She retrieved a handful from the box and waved them in front of her, announcing that the test was to be administered within the next couple of months.

"We will go over several of the previous exams to give you an idea of what the test will be like." Miss Ayers strolled the row of desks, stopping at each with the box. "Here are sample tests from previous years. If you want to do really well, take as many of these as you like, and study at home. There are plenty to go around."

When she came to me, I shuffled through the papers for as many previous years as I could find. Outside of school, my mission in life became to learn any possible question and answer that might appear on the Ohio Achievement Test. I took as many tests as I could.

After several months, the day of the test arrived. I took my seat. My diligence paid off. The questions were similar in content and style to all the previous tests. I had no problem finishing. Gertrude, the girl I thought was my toughest competitor, sat two desks in front of me, still working.

Test scores had to be tallied by county and then compiled for the entire state. This meant a long wait for the results. I longed for them like I had longed for a record player in fifth grade. We reviewed in class for finals. I learned a new nervous habit, pencil tapping. The days ticked away.

The morning that Miss Ayers informed us that she had the test scores, I thought I would faint. Butterflies filled my stomach as she congratulated the entire class for their efforts. From her desk, she began announcing winners, starting with honorable mentions, and deliberately stretching her pauses between names to pique suspense as she moved up the list through Susan, who earned third place, to Gina, who placed second.

Was it possible?

Miss Ayers called my name. She asked me to come to the front of the room. I walked up and stood next to her desk. My teacher pointed to the paper in front of her and, beginning at the bottom of the page, ran her finger up the entire page until she stopped at the name at the top.

"Class, Joann Campomizzi placed first and wins the ten-dollar top prize."

This was no monumental feat among my classmates; few paid much attention as I returned to my seat. But I rode home on a cloud that day, delighted to tell Mom of my triumph. She did not know what the Ohio Achievement test was, but she was happy because I was happy. I had to wait for Dad to wake up for work in order to tell him that I had placed first in Carroll County, but

I knew, I just knew, that he would be proud of me. We attended the next PTA meeting where the winners were invited on stage to receive their prizes. I glowed in the wealth a ten-dollar bill promised, quite a tidy sum. We showed all the signs of a happy family.

At home, however, the task was much more difficult. The rages, which still chronically toppled my father's otherwise serene disposition, terrified Lucy and me. Mom would try to intervene in order to calm him down, but his emotional wounds had cut too deep. We tried to understand, but looking back, I realize we were trying to absolve him of a horror that not even he could justify. In school I learned the facts and figures of a civilized world and how to become, hopefully, a productive member of society. But within the walls of home, I learned what I lived. Often the two worlds clashed, and for all my love for learning, I could not learn to reconcile the differences between the two.

Mother became more protective of our reputation in the community. What occurred at home remained at home. The consummate seamstress, she fashioned what each of us was expected to wear in the presence of others. I learned along the way to hide myself, that the real me was unacceptable to society at large.

I began high school in the fall of 1962 in a brand-new Catholic school in Carrollton, southeast of Malvern: St. Edward's. Twenty-four students comprised the first freshman class, including a half-dozen of us from Malvern. In four years we would become the first graduating class. Our courses included English, history, mathematics, and Latin, along with my two favorites: physical science and religion. Oddly, my green algebra book, a pilot program from the University of Illinois, surprised me. I had never seen a paperback textbook before.

I dove into my studies with no doubt of my ability to do well. I had looked forward to new friendships, but most of these through high school grew no deeper than acquaintances. In general I chalk this up to the geographic distances between towns, and in particular to the stigma I acquired as a teacher's pet. Deep inside I fancied the status, though it chafed a little.

During my freshman and sophomore years, I joined the cheerleaders for the school basketball team, the Knights. Both years I won the cheerleading finals, even though I couldn't jump. I *really* couldn't jump. Teachers sat as judges and I am sure I won because of my excellent grades. Rumors flew. *How does Joann win top spot when she can't even jump?* They did not say it to me, but I knew they were saying it, and I knew they were right.

Senior year the faculty chose me as May Queen. It was quite an honor. I wondered why I had been chosen but, deep down, I suspected that marks and my cloak of modesty that Mother insisted on had something to do with it. She was present for the affair and pleased indeed. I walked down the main aisle of the church in the presence of the entire student body, faculty, family members, and friends with a tiara of flowers to crown a statue of the Virgin Mary. It made me proud to be seen as humble.

Early in the season during my second year of high school, I arrived at games with my legs peppered by fleabites, a gift from my cat that we blithely let wander the fields outside our house one day. I unfolded my socks and pulled them up as far up my legs as I could, with a noticeable effect. I looked different from the rest of the girls, thus drawing even more attention to myself than did the rash I was trying to hide. I eventually listened to our head cheerleader and folded my socks.

I attended school functions, but I did not participate in what teens considered fun. I did not go to parties. When my friends arrived at school on Mondays and shared their experiences, I had not been part of them. I buried myself in study, absolutely convinced that my intellectual honesty would guide me through life, defying the emotional dishonesty churning away inside of me, laying bare the lie.

More often than not I found myself holding contradictory selves: the expressive, volatile, sometimes angry self I'd known as a child, and the succeesful, conformist, reasonable, and pure young woman I was scolded into being. A statue of Minerva.

And in many ways it was the same with my peers. I gave a façade of warmth and friendliness eager to meet new friends yet never did open up, terrified that they would discover the true me if I ever spoke openly and honestly.

And then there was the conflict between the expectations of home life and the expectations of social life, often in conflict with each other. After school, the bus would drop off several of my classmates at four corners in town where they gathered for sodas or pizza. Mother insisted that I come straight home.

By my junior year in high school, everyone was dating except me. I was friendly with all of the boys — just another one of the guys, the one they came to when they had a problem. I was not interested in dating any of them until a transfer student, Conrad, arrived at St. Edward's from out of state. Conrad had a crush on me. I felt the same way toward him, but feigned utter indifference. He was the only guy in our class who had a driver's license and a car. He often drove his brand-new Chevy to school.

One weekday evening, Conrad drove three of our friends and me to the big city of Canton and its large public library to work on our English research papers. They were due in six weeks. I chose psychiatry as my topic. The group spent a couple of hours reading reference books and copying notes onto three-by-five index cards. We checked out the books we could, knowing that they were due in two weeks.

On the way home, the girls coaxed me into sitting next to Conrad. I protested and pretended I didn't want to but did it anyway. He tried to hold my hand, but I pulled it away. Inwardly, I was thrilled, but outwardly I acted as if I didn't care. After all, I was under the edict of my faith and my upbringing. Serious dating simply wasn't an option. Neither could I ignore the watchful eye of my mother, who chaperoned all of the social events at school.

And there was never any question at home concerning my education. My parents took it as unalterable that I would continue on. Dad never finished college. I always believed that I would make him proud by finishing my education with a degree.

Above all else, I knew this, and I was determined to keep my marks up, come what may.

These were the days of John F. Kennedy's presidency. As Catholics, we were proud of his success and, like so many in the country, stunned by his death. But his legacy lived on. Our new high school adopted as its motto a line from the President's inaugural address: "God's work must truly be our own." We took the words as a challenge. Ads on TV promoted the newly founded Peace Corps and I dreamed of working as a doctor in far-off lands. Several of the boys in our class were considering the priesthood; one of the girls, a vocation as a nun; a couple of others intended to attend nursing school.

Our little towns raised us. They were no more than crossroads with a lumberyard, restaurant, tavern, drugstore, grocery store, and funeral parlor. Life grew through us like seed into the wheat and corn we ran through as children. And we too wanted to feed a hunger.

Gradually we finished our high school years. I graduated from St. Edward's in May 1966. My yen for competition drove me to do my best, and I expected this to fulfill my desires. I knew that from now on I would be sharing classes with students from more prestigious schools. I just decided to push myself all the harder. I had acquired a love for chemistry and decided to major in it in college.

During the summer months in the farm country of Ohio, lightning bugs salt the nights of June and July. As we grew up, through every conceivable dimension, from ground level to treetop, from near to far, their telegraphic yellow flashes of dots and dashes pierced the lightless dark of our little universe like stars through space. We never knew from where the next flash would come. Their brilliance would often shock our eyes, which constantly tried to readjust to the darkness. It was great fun, and the intense difference between night and light made you realize how dark the dark was, and how a little bit of light could blaze like life itself.

In just the same way, in the daylight of my ambition to absorb as much savvy as I could in school, I paid little attention to the humble little flashes of skill I was learning at home until I was asked to be a bridesmaid in a friend's wedding.

Carol had graduated from high school four years ahead of me, but we had attended grammar school together. She had been a regular visitor to our home, as Mother had made all of her cheerleading outfits throughout high school. Mom held Carol in high regard. One snowy afternoon in March 1966, as Mom and I finished lunch, I answered a knock at the kitchen door. Carol stepped through the back door with two bolts of fabric and patterns for her wedding gown and bridesmaid's dresses. Mom stood smiling by the red and chrome kitchen table in her flowered housedress with an ingenious look in her eyes, ready for a challenge.

"Hi, Mrs. Campomizzi, where do you want me to put these?"

"Here . . ." Mom took the bolts of fabric, along with the patterns, and set them on the red countertop. "Sit down for a minute, then I'll take your measurements." She opened the pattern for the wedding gown and began unfolding it on the kitchen table. "Let's see what we have here. The gown . . . dress for your sister as maid of honor . . . and we're sewing two bridesmaid's dresses, yes?"

"Yes." Carol sat, shifting back and forth in a gingham sheath. "My mother and the girls will be here in about half an hour."

I leaned over the counter, which separated the dining area from the kitchen, skimming the remaining patterns. "When is the wedding?"

"June 25th, in Columbus." Carol smiled at me with a hint of curiosity. She stood up and stepped back just a bit from the table, as though she was trying to get a broader view of the pattern. Blond hair the color of wheat ripening in the summer sun fell to her shoulders and danced on her checkered sheath. This slender woman of tamed fire almost bounced with an energy that seeped from the wellsprings of humanity and flowed through every pulse of her character. Her perpetual smile seemed to be forever on the verge of spilling into laughter, and often did.

"We have plenty of time for the sewing and the fittings." Mom studied the pattern in front of her, appraising lines on paper that she knew she could turn into a flowing work of art.

I stood at the counter, quietly admiring the scene. I was happy for Carol. I expected nothing less. One of the most popular girls at Malvern High, she had been head cheerleader and homecoming queen in her senior year and went on to graduate from college and become a math teacher. Carol's pace along the length of the table slowed deliberately, her eyes on Mother and the pattern. She seemed deep in thought. As if on a cue, the girl I thought of as having it all crossed from the table to the counter, leaned down to meet me eye to eye, and took my hand.

"Joann, I'm wondering if you could help me with something."

In a small town, everyone knows everyone, and I knew Carol like I knew my fondest dreams, as an ideal yet to be fulfilled. She represented everything I hoped for in my own life.

"Jim is Catholic. I am not. I learned during our marriage preparation classes that to be married in his faith, I must have at least one bridesmaid in the wedding party who is Catholic. I don't have close friends who are Catholic. I'd like to ask you to be in my wedding."

My mood soared. I did not expect the sense of elation that poured through me. I squeezed her hand. All that I could do was bite my lip and nod. Mom turned on the heel of her hand, tipped her head, and smiled at me over Carol's shoulder.

"Joann . . ." She held up the pattern envelope with the bridesmaid's picture and smiled. "What do you think?"

By the time Mom finished measuring us, Carol's mother and the girls had arrived. Mom took all of the initial measurements and arranged with the girls for the several fittings she would need by the end of May.

The Thursday before the wedding, Carol's parents picked me up for the two-hour drive to Columbus. Her sister, Nancy, Karen (a family friend attending the affair), and I all knew each other. We had arranged to share a room at a local hotel — for me the only time I ever stayed in a hotel but for the one night in Naples before my family left Italy. We settled in and all gathered for dinner at a restaurant. I watched what the others did and imitated them, because I had only eaten once in a restaurant since coming to America twelve years before.

On Friday, we relaxed and spent the afternoon around the pool, then dressed for the rehearsal at 6 p.m., with a dinner arranged afterward at the groom's home. The rehearsal went as planned. The priest offered a few words of final direction to Carol and Jim for the ceremony the next day and assured them that the wedding would flow smoothly. As we left the church, I stepped in next to Carol's mother to ask her about something I noticed during the rehearsal.

"I've only been to one other wedding in my life, so I don't know the customs. Are there usually the same number of bridesmaids as groomsmen?"

"Yes, Joann." She looked at me with a rather questioning smile. "That's pretty much the way of things."

"I was just wondering . . . there is one more groomsman than there are bridesmaids."

Carol's mother stopped in her tracks and made some quick, silent calculations. "How in heaven's name could we not have seen it?" She raised an arm as if to halt the exit of the bridal party from the church but thought better of it and answered me with an ironic twist in her voice. "The funny thing is that Karen would be happy to be in the wedding. Your mother gave me the pattern and the unused material, but we have no dress."

Carol learned the news at the rehearsal dinner. She took the setback with calm, nobly resigned to what she would have to do. I had been thinking. I leaned over toward Carol's mom.

"I think I can do this."

"What?"

"Make a bridesmaid's gown."

"By tomorrow?"

"I asked Jim's mom. She had a sewing machine, scissors, and everything I needed."

"I don't think you'll be able to do it. Even if you could, you're in the wedding. You'll be worn out."

"I'm willing to try."

Karen, having been rediscovered in the shuffle of wedding attendants, was as anxious for the challenge as I. Carol's mother retrieved the pattern and the material from her car. The guests left. Karen remained for measurements. Jim's parents went to bed, leaving the dining room table for laying out the material and pattern pieces. I set to the cutting, pinning, basting, measuring, and sewing, with Karen standing by for repeat fittings. By midnight, I had enough of the gown measured for her to get back to the motel and get some sleep.

In the Genesis account of creation, at the end of each day, God looked at what He had made and saw that it was good. At four o'clock on a Saturday morning in June of 1966, I had come the closest in my life to what He must have felt when he created the world and saw that it was good. I rolled onto a nearby sofa and slept until someone woke me to eat.

The groom's father drove me back to the hotel with the dress. I delivered the dress to Karen, slept for a couple more hours, and when I woke again I checked with Karen for any final adjustments. Then I dressed for the wedding. It made little difference to me how tired I may have felt. The bridal party made our procession to the front of the church. Karen's gown looked identical to the others. Jim and Carol exchanged their vows: he lean and gallant, she never more beautiful.

At the reception I discovered how tired I really was. I could not stay awake unless I kept dancing. By the time we returned to our rooms, I had lost all conception of time. I knew nothing until midmorning Sunday when I heard Nancy up and about getting ready for our trip home.

Parents and the bridal party all gathered for a farewell breakfast. The wedding, and the appearance of a fourth bridesmaid's dress, filled the conversation like the aroma of sausage and hotcakes filled the air, and I relished the flavor of that morning and the praise that came with it. On the way home, Carol's father promised me a steak dinner for my efforts. Good to his word, several weeks after the wedding, he and his wife, Carol's sister, and I dined at a restaurant in Canton. We all ordered steaks. I did not have the heart to tell them that I had never eaten a steak before, so I just had to watch them and learn how it was done.

I was eighteen years old. Graduation set the course for my future. The course had been set years before by the words of my grandfather on his front porch in the mountains of Italy—work hard in America, and any dream is possible. As a young adult in the summer of 1966, I felt his words to be true.

PART TWO:

AFTER THE FALL

CHAPTER 11

THE FALL

"Where am I, and why am I wearing this ugly hospital gown?" I shouted. "How did I get here?"

I didn't know how long I'd been sleeping, but I was fully awake now.

"You're in your room in Mercy Hospital." I looked up and saw a petite, blue-eyed, blond-haired woman who spoke with a soft voice. She must have been around forty-five years old.

"Who are you?" I asked. I didn't fully understand why, but I sensed that there was something seriously wrong with me.

"I am Gladys, your day nurse. I've been taking care of you." Gladys held a glass of water in one hand and a couple of pills in the other. "You are here recovering from a bad fall. You probably suffered a concussion. At least that's what they're treating you for. At twenty, you are the youngest patient in the psychiatric department."

"The psychiatric department! How long have I been here?"

"You have been here for several days." My nurse sat down on a wooden chair next to my bed. It was a room no larger than a dorm room. She crossed her legs and rested her chin on her hands.

"How did I get here?"

"Your mother and father admitted you. Do you remember where you were when you fell?" The pale light of the room melted into her white uniform as she pressed her lips between phrases. "It is important that you recall as many of the details as possible of what happened following your accident." She paused and straightened in her chair. "Can you tell me what you remember?"

"What can I remember?" I knew there was a chronicle of facts, a series of events, which led to this hospital bed, facts which for the life of me I could not piece together.

January 3, 1968. I was in my room in Marian Hall at the College of Steubenville, Ohio.

Judy, my roommate, and I had just returned from Christmas break to our small dorm room: two beds, a pair of desks, closets, and windows that looked out on a grass quadrangle off to the side of the campus. Judy had become a good friend — proud of her Hungarian heritage, and sure of what she wanted to do with her future. She was sweet, thin, and always well-dressed. We were both science majors and spent a lot of our time together.

Judy and I had been in our room only a short time when the phone down the hall rang. No one answered it. Finally, Judy said she would go answer it.

"You still have to unpack. I'll get it." I ran down the hallway and was still running as I turned the corner and reached for the phone on the wall. I missed and slipped on a puddle of melted snow. I fell flat on my back, striking my head on the floor. I saw a flash of bright twinkling lights but quickly got up. I didn't think anything serious had occurred. Several girls in nearby rooms heard me hit the floor, ran to my rescue, and walked me back to my room, trying to make sure I was okay. I told them I just wanted to rest. It was only four o'clock in the afternoon. I crawled under the covers, pulled them over my head, and slept until five the next morning. I felt wide awake and finished my chemistry and calculus homework. A few minutes late, I rushed to class.

I walked into class at 8:15 a.m. and handed the professor my homework. "Good morning, Professor, sorry I'm late." The reticent chemist rolled his eyes to signal his displeasure.

I went to the rest of my classes, not really giving any thought to my fall the previous afternoon.

But I found I could not concentrate. I didn't sleep that night, or the next, or the night after that. In fact, the night of the fall was the only full night's sleep that I was to get for a couple of weeks. Thoughts raced around in my head. My actions became sporadic and disconnected. Friends and professors noticed and began to question my unpredictable speech and behavior. No one related this to my fall. Something was changing within my mind, as if its walls were caving in all around me.

Late one night, several days after my fall, I went to the lounge on the same floor to study. I studied because I could not sleep. I was beyond exhaustion. When I went to leave a couple of hours later, I grabbed the doorknob and could not open it. Somehow, the lock on the doorknob had jammed when I entered.

"Let me out of here!" I screamed. Panic struck. I knocked on the door. "Can anyone hear me?" It was three o'clock in the morning; no one answered. I didn't know whether to yell to get attention or to keep quiet because of the hour. The clock on the wall trickled minutes that spilled into hours.

I must have napped on and off. In and out of half-sleep, a slow rising swell of exuberance surged into euphoria. I became convinced that God was in the room with me, only to quickly crash down into dark black clouds of depression. In the clutch of a cryptic confusion, my world slipped in and out of a torture of pain, sleeplessness, and anguish. I experienced intensely that night, for the first time, a theme that would continue with me for decades to follow, staggering rises and falls between ecstasy and despair, wondering where the pain was coming from.

It could not be from God, I reasoned. He offers peace and tranquility. Then was it I? Mercifully, morning arrived, the sun rose, the pain dissipated. I still could not open the door.

I felt excited and wide awake, as if I were the only person that God was concerned about, if indeed He was not dead (I couldn't make up my mind). By 7 a.m. I tried the door again. It was still locked. I leaned against it, whispering, "Let me out of here. Will someone let me out?"

Judy woke up, and not finding me in bed, went looking for me. She came to the lounge, opened the door, and rushed in. She put her arms around me.

"What's the matter? What's going on here?"

"I don't know, I don't know, I don't know what is happening to me. I'm scared." I started to cry.

"You're not the same since you fell."

She walked me back to our room and then to my classes. At the end of the day, Judy and Marsha, a mutual friend and an

English major, escorted me to the cafeteria. Afterward I returned to my room. I knew I would not be able to sleep again. I did not want to keep Judy awake, so I once again left for the lounge, my sanctuary of solitude where I could be alone, and stayed awake with my thoughts for another night.

One of the Franciscan priests, my spiritual advisor, was the first to make the connection between my fall and the lack of sleep. He gave me a business card with the name and phone number of Dr. White, a psychologist with an office in downtown Steubenville.

"You should go and talk with her." We had just finished his theology class and were walking toward my dorm down one of the two hills on which the college was built. "I think she will be able to help you."

I returned to the dorm, called, and made an appointment from the only phone on the floor, the one I had fallen near.

The following afternoon I arrived a few minutes early. Dr. White was the only person in the room. Tall, dark-haired, and soft-spoken, she smiled, stepped out from behind her desk, and introduced herself in a motherly voice. I smiled a timid hello and gazed around her office, captivated. It was lush with memorabilia from her travels around the world and furnished with elegant brown leather furniture. Wood-paneled walls, rich and dark, were very unlike the spartan culture of home and school. I was stunned by the opulence. I suddenly remembered her presence, and the spell broke.

Dr. White put her hand on my shoulder, looked at me, and smiled. "I worked for all of this." She pulled up a chair and sat down close to me. "I've heard you fell and things haven't been the same since."

I had to trust her. I didn't know where else to turn.

Dr. White asked several questions, most focusing on when I fell. Did I see stars? Did I get up right away? Did I fall asleep right after I fell? I nodded a yes to each of them. She concluded that the symptoms were related to the accident and advised me to see a medical doctor, either a local physician or my own doctor at home, but to do it as soon as possible.

I never made an appointment because I felt that I wanted to go home and see Dr. Stires, our family physician, and I missed my family.

Weeks later, I found myself in the psychiatric wing of a hospital. I was telling Nurse Gladys the story of how I fell as I ran down the hall in my dormitory — trying to remember, picking up bits and pieces of a life that had fallen, was broken and shattered.

"It's quite a thing to go through," Gladys said with genuine sympathy, and jotted down a couple of notes. "Did you fall asleep immediately after you fell?" I tried to remember. She inquired about my lack of sleep in the days that followed. I tried to remember. The more questions she asked, the more anxious I became. Sensing my restlessness, she told me that we would continue the following day. "You're very confused. Your doctor sent you to us because he believes that we can help to clear up the confusion. Dr. Beshara is very well-known and respected in this community. He will give you the best available medical care."

Gladys handed me two pills and a glass of water. I took a sip of water and heard my father's deep voice in the hallway. His voice — at times as sweet and mellow as soft rain on a wooden porch, at others as violent as a wind-driven downpour — filled me with both hope and fear.

My mother and father entered the room. I immediately began crying.

"Why are you so upset?" my mother asked with a worried smile. She wrapped her arms around me and tried as best she could to console me, but I continued to cry. My father stood behind her in awkward silence.

"What makes you think you can help me?" I twisted the words between sobs.

My mother looked at the ceiling and my father paced, neither sure of what to say. They tried to distract my attention from this bad dream turned real, but they were as confused as I was.

I was deeply distressed about my future and whether I would be able to return to college. I asked about what would happen in the future. My mother told me she was making me a new red dress to wear for the day I came home. She thought that looking good would help me. "We're glad this is a Catholic hospital," she said, gazing at a crucifix on the hospital-green wall above the bed. "We are praying for your recovery."

My father needed a cigarette and stepped out of the room nearly as quickly as he came in. His experiences during World War II had wiped out any tolerance for the surreal.

Mother remained with me, although she appeared to be uncomfortable with the surroundings. She cast an occasional smile in my direction, but her eyes would drift off, searching the floor and corners of the room, trying to find somewhere to hide from the wooden silence. Father returned about fifteen minutes later. The silence deepened. The anguish of not knowing what was happening to me combined with the humiliation of having sunk my parents' dreams made the silence unbearable. I couldn't take the buried feelings anymore. I was always expected to be a perfect child, at least publicly. What would happen now?

"What kind of treatment is Dr. Beshara going to perform on me? What do I have?"

"Joann, you need to be here because of your accident." My father stood by the door, looking into my eyes. I knew he could relate to whatever was happening to me, though confusion laced the compassion in his voice. "This hospital has the best medical help for head injuries in this area."

"We are only trying to protect you." I could hear the misleading tone in my mother's voice. "That's why we are not telling any of our family, friends, and neighbors. You will have to trust us."

I could not control my rage. "No, the fact that this beautiful and intelligent daughter of yours, or so you say, who was majoring in chemistry is now in the psychiatric wing of the hospital is not something you want published in the *Malvern Community News*, is it?"

The two most important people in my life responded with stony silence.

I sat in that hospital, staring into nothing, wondering how I was supposed to trust a mother and father who would not tell anyone that I had a head injury. It was an accident. I did not will it to happen or cause it. If only that puddle of melted snow had not been on the floor. If only I had walked. But I could not turn back time. It was what it was. And it was an outrage.

A crushing loneliness appeared as if I was in one world, they in another, and there was nothing I could do to get through to them.

My parents stayed a couple more hours. Sugary clichés about getting well sprinkled the unbearable silence. The worst part was that they seemed embarrassed at having to be there. As they left, I felt a deepening sense of shame. I broke down again and cried. I tried to make sense of the last three weeks of my life, three weeks I couldn't remember well. For my own sanity, I had to remember, but I could only recall fragments.

CHAPTER 12

MERCY HOSPITAL

In the early hours, several mornings a week, a nurse arrived at my bedside. "It's time to wake up." She would give me a gentle nudge. "Joann, wake up, you can sleep later."

Joann doesn't want to wake up. She just wants to sleep. It is 4 a.m.

I was taken on a gurney to the modest treatment room where Dr. Beshara was waiting, sitting on a stool next to the breadbox-sized machine.

"Concentrate on my glasses," the doctor said, bending over as he prepared a dose of ECT. I stared through his horn-rimmed glasses into his stoic eyes.

I believed that his intentions were sincere and these treatments would help me get better, but what he was doing was agony.

The doctor set the voltage.

"Dr. Beshara, how can you do this?" I pleaded. "Please don't do this to me."

"I know this is intense, Joann. I'll make it as short as I can." He flipped the switch. Pain shot through me. My body stiffened. I gritted my teeth. My hands clenched into clubs. Electricity flowed through my nerves to my brain. In seconds my body received enough voltage to cause a seizure.

The lightning lasted only for a matter of seconds. The flow of electrons through my body stopped as abruptly as it began. My fists loosened. The treatment was over for today, but there would be others. The pain temporarily ended, but the memory endured.

The nurse wheeled me back to my room and rolled me from the gurney back to my bed. I was spent with pain and exhaustion, somewhere close to the borders of my life, somewhere between consciousness and delirium, between reason and chaos. Blood flowed back into my hands. My fingers relaxed and slowly opened like flowers. In and out of myself, I closed my eyes and slept for several hours.

"Wake up. It's time for your bath." The nurse came in every other day. "Get your bathrobe and clothes and come with me."

"I don't know what I want to wear."

"Pick out something. You have ten minutes."

A group of women and a group of men were already waiting in the hallway when we arrived. Long, opaque curtains labeled *Men* and *Women* surrounded the tubs of the communal baths, a single room with three tubs for the men and three for the women. I wore a bathrobe and underwear surrounded by one of the curtains. As a young girl, I was extremely modest, so I was humiliated as I took off my clothes with the sound of male voices just beyond the curtains. I got in the tub and rushed my bath, hurrying to get it over with, terrified that someone would see me. My nurse waited outside the curtain. She handed me a white towel, I got out of the tub, dried myself off, and quickly dressed. Baths were a humiliation.

My body was clean but my soul was dirty. Dear God, what had I done to deserve this? If my parents knew how I was being treated, what would they say?

I visited with some of the other female patients. They were at least twice my age and didn't like the hospital any more than I did. I did not converse long with them. I cowered back to my room, bathed in guilt and shame, trying to convince myself that I was too young to be going through this.

Dear God, I feel so worthless. How many other people will find out that I am in here?

I considered myself damaged goods, and as far as I was concerned, so did my family. *God, why don't you just let me die? I just want to die. Please put an end to this pain.*

Secret — my pain had to be a secret. My mother had asked, "What will the neighbors think?" I sank deeper and deeper into my depression. I was trying to escape it but couldn't. The pain dug deep into my soul. *Is this hell?*

I spent a total of three weeks in the hospital.

CHAPTER 13

I AM FREE

When I was discharged, Dr. Beshara scheduled a follow-up office visit for me a couple of weeks later. During that visit, he told my mother that if I lost twenty pounds, I would be all right—as if the weight that I carried around was physical. I was presenting what the good doctor wanted to see, and I was succeeding. He gave me my walking papers, no pills, no medication, no more appointments. I was out the door.

I remember the sun was shining, but I was still in a deep depression. My parents kept my hospital stay a secret, and that increased the intensity of my anguish as well as my pain and guilt. They didn't understand the psychological ramifications of their secrecy. *Would they ever?* I wondered.

Home from Mercy Hospital, I prayed every day that the agony would pass. *Will I ever be successful?* I saw no hope. It was doomsday. Would I ever go back to college or take any chemistry courses, the ones I loved the most, or any of the others that would lead me to medical school?

I had fallen into a deep hole out of which I could not climb. I still dreamed of living life to the fullest, but the injury, the illness, the treatment—I didn't know which—had shattered my self-confidence. Oh, how I wanted to be normal and leave these problems behind. I longed for the black cloud over my head to disappear. I turned to God continually, confused.

One night, I sat at my parents' kitchen table and looked through the windows to the stars. Magnificent and beautiful, they twinkled in the sky. All I could think of was that God created all of this. The air was still and cool. For a moment, I was at peace, in awe of His creation. Yet my parents' reticence haunted these silent moments. An isolating fear of guilt echoed through my thoughts, guilt that perhaps I did something to cause this. I would repeat this dozens of nights in the months ahead.

It was 2 a.m. The restlessness returned. I walked over to the sink, drank a glass of water, paced around the kitchen, walked down the hall, and peeked into our bedroom. My sister was sound asleep. I heard my mother and father in their bedroom, deep in conversation. My mother accidently dropped her mirror on the hardwood floor.

Smettere di farecosi tanto rumore! "Stop making so much noise!" My father's deep voice echoed down the hallway, accompanied by the scent of cigarettes.

I returned to the kitchen. My mother's footsteps were close behind as she tiptoed down the short hallway to the kitchen. Her eyes were heavy. She looked exhausted, as reluctant a visitor to the kitchen as she was an immigrant to America—a choice she made to please her husband. Dressed in a pink flannel nightgown and matching nightcap, she was a fashion doyenne, even in the middle of the night, a vestige of the days when she had worked with many dress designers in Italy.

I walked past her and made my way back to the kitchen window. Her happiness revolved around taking care of my sister and me, her dignity around our success. *She must be very disappointed in me.* Standing next to the long red countertop, she took a bag of bleached white wheat flour down from the cupboard.

There wouldn't be any solitude in these wee hours tonight. I craved the solitude, to be alone with my thoughts and God, but my mother wouldn't leave me alone. She chirped snippets of conversation as she worked the flour into dough, clearly worrying about me, wanting to help, but not knowing how. In time, she shuffled over to the window and looked out over me into the night sky.

"Joann, why don't you get some sleep?"

I didn't answer. Leaning over the table, she was so close it felt as though she were peering into my thoughts.

"Will you listen to me just once in your life? You've always been difficult, but now, in the state you're in, you need to do as I say."

I went to bed.

My mother followed me, touched my face, and put her arms around me. Pulling the bedcovers over me, she held me very tightly and I drifted off to sleep.

For the next six months we played this tug-of-war. I was twenty, and I had been diagnosed with clinical depression. I tried to look ahead, but I no longer knew what to look for.

After six months as a recluse during what should have been the second semester of my sophomore year at college, I persuaded my parents to let me return to Steubenville for summer school.

I enrolled in an intermediate Spanish class and a course in moral theology. I took the classes in the morning, ate, and slept the rest of the day. It was an effort to get out of bed. I socialized with no one. I managed to pass both courses.

In September of 1968, I returned for what should have been my junior year at Steubenville. Mom and Dad drove me down. I was still not fully recovered from my fall and I did the best I could. I carried a regular academic load and did average work, but I spent most of my time outside of class in my dorm, either working on assignments or sleeping. Many of my friends from my freshman year had transferred to other schools and life was not the same. The friends I made were academic acquaintances, and even in their midst I felt separate from them. At a small school in a small city, it seemed as though everyone knew what had happened to me, that I had become the secret they kept from me. By December, I was ready to transfer too.

I transferred to Walsh College in North Canton, Ohio, in January of 1969, majoring in chemistry. It is a small Catholic college governed by Christian Brothers. I had completed my application, mailed it in, and had my transcripts sent. This process also required me to have an interview with Brother Conrad, a faculty member.

The day of my appointment at Walsh is very vivid in my mind. Brother Conrad left the room for a few minutes and left my folder on the desk next to me. My curiosity got the better of me and I took a peek. I read that I was an excellent student but that at times I was emotionally inconsistent. At first I resented what it said, then I agreed. I quickly closed the folder and waited for Brother Conrad to return. Upon his return, we had an hour-long conversation. It must have satisfied him because at the end he said: "Everything is very good, Joann, and I welcome you to Walsh College."

From January 1969 until the beginning of my senior year, I lodged with a widow who worked with my mother, helping to cook and care for her four children. It was a wonderful experience. A couple of Walsh classmates gave me a ride every day. Life was good.

My fall and its aftermath had stripped me of my ability to function for six months, costing me the first semester of my junior year. To make up for it, I took on a heavy course load including an organic chemistry class. The students were all men except for me and one other girl.

I still carried my high school dream of becoming a doctor in Africa. Now, with semi-independence, the idea struck me as possible. I picked up an application from school to join the Peace Corps. One weekend visiting home, I showed my mother the completed form and told her what it was. She took one look at the form, another at me.

"You don't need to go anywhere to help people. You can help your own family."

With those few words, my mother crushed my dreams. She had a very strong influence over my decision to not join the Peace Corps. My future would be changed forever. I was crushed and disappointed at my mother's answer. I really wanted to join the Peace Corps but emotionally I could not because my mother did not approve, and I needed for her to approve.

I threw myself into my studies and my grades reflected it. I made new friends. We talked about our lives. I did not mention my fall and what followed. I blocked out that part of my life. I almost forgot my stay at Mercy Hospital. I smiled a lot. I would have to spend an extra year in college to make up for courses I missed and credits that would not transfer from Steubenville, but that was fine with me. Life was good.

In August of 1970, just before the start of my senior year, the principal at Brunnerdale High School Seminary in Canton called to ask me to interview for a part-time position teaching chemistry.

I passed the interview and began teaching chemistry at Brunnerdale from 7:30 to 8:30 a.m., Monday through Friday. It was only a fifteen-minute drive from Walsh; I could teach and still make it to my first class. I didn't know until the interview that my college advisor and physics professor, Brother Simeon — a warm, round, balding middle-aged man with the patience of Job — had recommended me. I was being drawn toward a path I had never before considered. I would discover that I loved teaching.

My father convinced me to buy a brand-new Buick for my first car. Beginning in September of 1970, I lived at home and drove back and forth to college and to my teaching job. I could now give my mother a ride to work. I had to teach my class an hour before she started work, so I dropped her off at St. Peter's Church to attend morning Mass. During the half-hour trip each way, she spoke to me about weather, work, clothes, or cooking. I listened to her, spoke when expected to. The rest of the time I buried myself in my teaching position, school, and even took on duties as editor of the college yearbook and vice president of the senior class. The past was dead and gone.

Then Bill came into my life.

I met him at one of our college dances when my friend Kathy pointed him out. To my surprise, he came over and asked me to dance. We saw each other at a college baseball game a week later and after that spent all our free time together. He began driving down to Malvern, about a forty-minute drive, every weekend.

One night, a couple of weeks before Christmas, my parents had gone shopping. Bill and I stood by the kitchen sink making small talk, chatting about nothing in particular, simply sipping the comfort of each other's company. His voice softened. The conversation slowed. He was searching for something, and I wanted to let him find it.

"I love you, and I want to marry you."

I jumped back with shock then grabbed him and hugged him.

"I love you too." This was the first time in my life that I trusted a guy enough to say it.

Bill had just uttered the happiest words I ever heard in my life. We stood next to the same window bearing the light of the same moon that shone over dozens of nights through months of recovery, when I had searched for meaning fewer than two years before. I had mentioned the accident to Bill but did not go into details. I feared losing him. Besides, as far as I was concerned, the event had passed. I had recovered and moved on. If memories of it rose to conscious thought, I willed them back to submission. But for all of my successes, for all I had accomplished, deep within me, beyond the depth of words, flowed a current of fear that I was broken, that something was wrong. And I could not shake the doubt. Now, with Bill by my side, I thought I could conquer anything.

We both graduated in May 1971, and that same month I was offered a full-time position at Brunnerdale teaching chemistry, physical science, and biology. I accepted and attended the University of Akron during the summer to take the courses required for an Ohio Temporary Teaching Certificate so I could begin teaching full time in September. We had assumed that Bill would look for a job in Canton, but Bill's mother had become seriously ill. He returned to Rochester, New York, his hometown, after graduation to spend time with his parents. He landed a job as an accountant in his uncle's accounting firm.

On June 19, 1971, his mother passed away. The news brought me to his hometown out of respect for him and his family. As I had met her only twice, I could only feel grief through the sorrow in the eyes of Bill and his family. I was twenty-three years old and deeply absorbed in my education and future. Death was a foreigner, an intruder into the land and vitality of the living, and I could only relate to it through Bill's eyes. Bill was more mature than I, with a deeper grasp of the totality of it all.

About the same time, Mom received a call from Italy from one of her sisters. Papa Domenico was ill and wanted to see her. Mother immediately flew to Italy to be with him.

When Papa Domenico died two months later, my mother resigned herself to it, much as when my little sister died in 1956. I think that I learned to accept it as she had. I have taken a lifetime to begin to see the gentle touch my grandfather left on my soul. His quiet, pensive presence in a room, like a seed in the womb of the earth, his love of learning, his undivided interest in my school work, the silent authority that dwelt in him, roam through my life like a benevolent king. I am an heir to his benevolence.

In August of 1971 I rented an apartment in Canton with two other girls, Marlane and Joanne, who were elementary school teachers. Mother got her daily ride to work with someone else. She kept her sorrow over her father's death to herself and continued to work and take care of her family.

I began teaching chemistry and physical science in September 1971 but struggled teaching biology. I studied and studied in order to learn the materials and bolstered my lack of experience with several school field trips to one of the local hospitals to learn from professionals applying biology in the real world.

Bill and I were married on June 10, 1972, in the chapel of Brunnerdale Seminary in a lavish ceremony that rivaled that in *The Sound of Music*. I had asked permission to be married in the chapel. Like an organ in a choir loft shaking the very foundation of its church, the staff pulled out all the stops and helped us celebrate our wedding with the pomp of royalty. Six priests officiated; two of my students, Larry and Tim, were altar boys; Brother Ben and a small group of boys from the seminary's choir provided the music. My father, dressed in a tuxedo with a white jacket and pink shirt that matched Bill's, was so proud as we began our walk down the white cloth-covered aisle to the altar. My mother stood with a polite smile in the left front pew between the altar and Bill, wearing the pink satin dress and coat that she had designed, her head held high. She was the designer and creator of my wedding gown and veil, also having designed my sister's rose-colored satin maid of honor gown, and the pink bridesmaid's gowns.

We had a lavish sit-down dinner at the Onesto Hotel in Canton, accompanied by wedding cake and the best champagne for the wedding reception. Afterward, Bill and I drove to Cleveland for a flight to Bermuda for our honeymoon. A sense of freedom and independence that I had never known before surged through me.

Newly married, in glorious weather on an island in the Atlantic, the world appeared bigger and more beautiful than I ever could have imagined.

Our intentions had been to live in Canton, but Bill was concerned over his father's declining health. Bill, an only child, did not want his father to be alone. I deferred to his wishes. We decided to start our new life in Rochester and I moved in with him and his father, Rocky. I was unhappy from the start. Don't get me wrong. Rocky was a nice, quiet man. But he didn't leave the house much. I had taken over the cooking to help out, but I often felt I was an interloper in the relationship between my husband and his father. I told Bill that I was unhappy, but he didn't seem to understand.

I found a job teaching seventh- and eighth-grade science at a nearby Catholic school, St. Thomas the Apostle, in September 1972. This eased the tension somewhat. I became pregnant in 1973, the same time that I started taking courses for my certification.

I needed some space for us, and Bill began to understand. In August, we rented an apartment the next street over and we all breathed a sigh of relief.

My provisional teaching certificate for New York State was only valid for five years, after which I would need a master's degree to be licensed to teach. My provisional certificate was only valid till 1977. I quit teaching in June 1973 and focused on raising a family and gradually studying toward my graduate degree. By 1978, my three children were born. I spent many hours after the kids were asleep and before they awoke studying and completing my assignments. I prided myself on the fact that my studies were not interfering with my family. When I needed to go to the library to do research, a neighbor, Mrs. Bain, would walk over to my house to take care of my children a couple of days a week. Since Mrs. Bain was a mother of five, I figured that Stephanie, Stacie, and Michael would be in good hands. I was determined to complete my education.

Stephanie was born on April 17 of 1974. She had beautiful pink skin and pitch-black hair flowing down her neck. I couldn't be happier. I prayed and prayed for another child. Twenty-three months later, in October 1976, Stacie Anne who sang and sang brought joy into our lives. In September of 1978, Michael, the biggest of them all, entered our world.

After Michael's birth, Bill went to see his father, who was critically ill, to deliver the good news. My father-in-law died the next day.

CHAPTER 14

SUMMER 1981

By May of 1981, I had finally earned my second degree. I received my Master of Science from Nazareth College on Mother's Day in the presence of my husband, my mother, and my daughters. Michael was too young to attend. I thought of my degree like an insurance policy. It was something I would use in the future when I returned to teaching. Yes, there were days that I wanted my career, but the majority of the time I enjoyed being a wife and mother. Bill was as relieved and happy as I that I had finished my formal education. We treated ourselves to a luscious dinner, and later, to top off the day, my family presented me with a food processor I had wished for as a graduation present.

Until August of 1981, I was living a pretty typical middle-class life, similar to the lives of thousands of other women in the world around me. We perceived our lives as happy — just what mothers did. We raised our children. Thirty-three years old, married and blessed with three beautiful children, I had no reason not to be happy.

Before my fall in college, all that I ever imagined concerned a career in a field of medicine. Afterward, I lost confidence in such a bold future. Now I was even losing confidence in returning to teaching. Was I failing my mission in life? I tried to reason away the deep sense of shame I felt since the head injury and hospitalization in 1968.

June and July of 1981 bustled with activity. Bill left to spend six weeks working out of town. Although he came home several weekends throughout the summer, we missed his presence and, like an ebbing tide, felt a part of us leaving with him each time he left. Right after our Fourth of July weekend together, Bill left for Andover. Stephanie, Stacie, Michael, and I packed our suitcases and loaded the car with favorite books and plenty of snacks for the six-hour trip to Canton to visit my family. The children chattered and played. I drove along the flat plains, orchards, and vineyards of Western New York to where the northern edge of the Allegheny Plateau rises above Lake Erie. We stopped for lunch at a McDonald's in Erie, the halfway point of our journey, and continued on in fine weather and on good roads without incident. Yet I could feel the tension rising in me, wondering what I was doing. Did I really want to go to Ohio for three weeks by myself with three small children? As a grown adult, the strain was even more evident between my mother and me. We were both strong-willed and found it hard to give in. It was difficult to agree on anything—what to cook, what to wear, whom to visit— but I had promised my parents and my sister.

The perpetual chant of "Are we there yet?" turned into cheers as we passed London's Candies on Main Street in North Canton on that hot July afternoon, then rounded the corner onto Hallum and down the street to my parents' house. We had the air conditioning running with the windows closed. I stepped out of the car to open the doors for the kids and caught the aroma of my mother's cooking. The smell of her homemade sauce drifted throughout the neighborhood.

Stephanie, Stacie, and Michael raced to the front door of the small Cape Cod house built of brick the color of red pine bark. Nona and Papa were waiting at the door and swept them in with hugs and kisses.

Mom was old school, making recipes she knew by heart since childhood for sauce, noodles, gnocchi, lasagna, and fried zucchini, using fresh tomatoes and zucchini from a garden she had planted along the front of the house. The garden was nothing compared to the huge one my father grew in Malvern—potatoes, green beans, peppers, tomatoes, and, far out in the yard, near the birdhouses, an apple tree and a peach tree. He had wanted to plant a small garden in North Canton, but by this time, Dad had been crippled with chronic arthritic gout for nearly five years, unable to work and struggling even to walk. Mother never drove. They had moved to North Canton in order to be closer to the department store where she worked. This relieved him of the half-hour drive each way back and forth from Malvern. I never knew until my mother, in her eighties, told me, but he used a cane to go for daily walks down to the grammar school at the end of their street, sit on the fence for a while, then walk home. Mom found out after Dad's death that a neighbor used to keep an eye on him as he lugged himself along the street to make sure he made it home okay.

My father wanted to work and tried to, but he could not manage even custodial work at a nearby school. One day during our visit in 1981, he asked me to walk around the block with him. I deeply enjoyed our time together, and I began to realize what he was going through. The handsome, demure man I longed to see at the Canton train station twenty-seven years before now fought for every step. Amid the small talk, he told me that Mom had to do the gardening because of the excruciating pain that had consumed his joints. He stopped and turned to look at me. He winked as he raised his right hand in a V for victory, with a cigarette between the fingers in his left hand. Dad touched my hand as he stopped and turned to look into my eyes with a smile that willed itself above his pain. I never once saw him use a cane.

Later that afternoon, our family sat down at the maple table in the kitchen for an early dinner of spaghetti, meatballs, and homemade Italian bread. Dad opened a bottle of beer, took out a cigarette, sat down with his clan, and we feasted. Some days Mom would bring out her utensils to make a batch of fresh pasta. The kids kneaded out the bread dough to bake their own homemade rolls so they could eat them fresh out of the oven.

These were times when I could try to relax. At times I would go out into the living room and try to read a book but I couldn't concentrate on words. I was possessed by the activity in the kitchen, keenly aware that this was an event for the grandchildren, an event to which I was not welcome.

One day, Dad came into the kitchen from his roost in the garden where he spent much of his time. I could hear the smile in his words when he asked the kids what they were doing.

Michael, the youngest, threw his hands up in the air, chalked with dough.

"We're making food!" The other two followed suit.

Dad laughed his congenial laugh and poked his head into the living room. "Jo, want to go for a ride?"

Dad drove us a couple of miles under the dry July sun to John's Bar on Cleveland Avenue. We perched on wooden stools at the bar. He ordered a beer. I had a cola with ice, the cold, tall glass sweating down onto a white napkin on the mahogany bar. At home we'd sit on one of the cinder block benches scattered around the backyard and chat about the weather or what Mom was growing in the garden. Sometimes he would call into the house for the kids to come out, and we would watch them play. At John's, Dad could just enjoy his solitude. He could strike up a conversation with anyone. He was an amiable guy, and at times like this, I would listen as he chatted with the owner or a customer he knew. Yet the talk would often be brief. He'd settle into the contentment of quiet with a bottle of beer and his cigarettes, with an occasional exchange between us. I didn't mind at all. I loved watching him at ease. In the anonymity of a place outside of the house, where I so often felt the inner tension of family life, I could watch him relax and be himself, the man beneath the wounds of his life. I was proud of him. I knew in my heart of hearts that he was a good man.

I thought of his days in Malvern. He loved his garden, often giving away half of what he grew to family, friends, or neighbors. Dad had constructed nestings, basically apartment houses on tall poles for martins, and placed them all over the backyard. The casual indifference of creatures to human affairs soothed him. His affection for our dogs and cats over the years, especially a black cocker spaniel named Shadow, revealed tenderness about him that he was rarely really able to show to humans. He trusted others; he didn't hold grudges. He never missed a day of work. There were days when I would walk out the back door of the house and just watch him in his garden, silent as a beast of burden, weeding and cultivating his way along rows of tomatoes, peppers, corn, zucchini, and green beans.

Mom made batches of bread and rolls about once a week. One of my earliest memories of Italy was of walking next to my mother, with my sister in her arms, as she took her dough to the oven in the town square to be baked in the communal oven. Now my children were learning. With her grandchildren in town, this became more of a project that usual. She would give each of them a ration of dough for kneading and shaping. Stephanie rolled hers into three long pretzel-like rods and braided them into a mini-loaf. Stacie watched and tried to do the same. Michael added his creation, a loaf with bumps. We had made bread at home before, so they knew what they had to do: place everything on a greased cookie sheet, cover with a damp kitchen towel, let the dough rise for an hour or so, then bake. The kids rattled around the house as they always did; the scent of warm water and sugar added to the yeast flowed through the air. They enjoyed their warm bread with butter as soon as it was baked.

Mom took as much time off work as she could during our visit, but she had to keep working. One morning, later in our visit, she asked me to make bread. I could do it blindfolded—five pounds of flour in a huge stainless steel bowl, water, yeast, a little sugar, salt, and some vegetable oil. I could have been home, or in North Canton, or Malvern. I had been making bread since I was ten years old.

Suddenly, I heard my father's laugh coming from the living room. It reminded me of when I was a girl of fourteen. I used to make a special bread for my father when he asked for or demanded it: flour, water, salt, no yeast, baked into a brick about an inch thick. When he laughed, his eyes smiled with the warmth and softness of fresh-baked bread. In his rages, I had never looked him in the eyes, terrified of what I would see.

My sister Lucy was a teacher and visited almost every day. The kids loved spending time with her. As they romped around the house, they routinely stopped at the front door in search of their aunt. The seven-year-old, five-year-old, and three-year-old peered through the window to see if she was pulling into the driveway. They knew they were going to have a blast with her. She hauled them off to the park for the swings and slides, drove them to a nearby arcade to play Pac-Man and all the latest video games, herded them two miles to Maxie's Drive-In where carhops indulged them with ice cream and root beer. They made regular pilgrimages on foot a very short distance to the corner of Hallum and Main to the coveted candy store. Sometimes she lingered after supper and let the girls play dress-up using our old prom gowns. Michael, not to be outdone or forgotten, strutted around the living room in a navy blue blazer of Dad's with gold buttons, proud enough to pop the buttons off, as if he were twenty years old.

At times during our visit, when Lucy led our little flock around North Canton and Mom wasn't working, Mom and I sat at the kitchen table, she and her sewing machine at one end and I with material and pattern at the other. Mother was still an excellent seamstress and a very creative dress designer, talents she often reminded me about not so much in words as in the art of dominance.

Mom selected three or four new patterns from her collection and asked me to pick one out that I liked. I might prefer yellow polyester for a pattern. She would choose a different pattern for the same material and then pick one for the gabardine that she had. We discussed the possibilities and eventually I deferred to her. I cut and pinned. She sewed and glanced over to see if I was keeping up with her.

The Wednesday before we left, Mom treated Stephanie, Stacie, and Michael to new outfits at Stern and Mann's, the high-end clothing store where she worked as a dress designer and seamstress. Like a queen entering her court, she paraded us from department to department, introducing everyone to her grandchildren, lauding me as the science teacher on sabbatical choosing to stay home and raise her children. Next came the shopping. I don't know who was more delighted, Mom or my little ones. The shopping trip to Stern and Mann's became a tradition that continued until the store closed its doors in the 1990s, over a century after opening them in 1887.

My parents had moved to North Canton in 1978, after my sister and I had graduated from college and moved out on our own. Other than the year I taught at Brunnerdale, I had no real ties in Canton. Malvern, Ohio, was my family home. Regardless of how deep the relationship with my sister and my parents was, after three weeks I was anxious to get back to my own home and the ways that were now my world. Papa and Nona would be glad to have us stay. They truly enjoyed being with their grandchildren. But I had entered the prime of my life. As much as I loved my parents, I needed to be free of them, to get back home, to show them and myself that I was an adult, fully capable of functioning on my own.

By the time we returned, Bill was already home. We spent the next week getting ready for our planned vacation to two amusement parks in the Adirondack Mountains: Enchanted Forest and The North Pole. I was exhausted from the trip to Ohio. The travel, keeping the kids busy, and the energy I needed to keep all activities in balance had worn me out. But I kept it to myself and did not tell Bill.

We settled in at a lodge near Lake Placid and would spend the next four days exploring every possible thrill for our three young adventurers. Bill went on almost every ride with them. I managed a small roller coaster ride with them, but felt dizzy and disoriented and couldn't wait to get off. I didn't ride another ride. I could feel some distant tinge of anxiety but dismissed it as a reaction to the ups and downs of the roller coaster. My consolation was a family photo taken of us in our personalized Santa hats.

We were three days into the trip, late morning one beautiful warm summer day. After Bill shuttled Stephanie and Stacie onto one of the rides they wanted to try for themselves, and while Michael explored the stones at our feet, he grabbed me by the arm and pulled me face-to-face with him.

"Are you all right?"

"What are you talking about?"

"What's going on with you? Don't you see what I see? You're acting like you're losing control. You act tired, you're irritable, and you're talking much faster than normal." He said it all in an angry whisper. "Get your act together." It wasn't a request.

I couldn't sleep that night. I had no idea that anything was wrong. When I was sure everyone was asleep, I got up and wandered the lobby of the lodge. Throughout my adult life I had used the strength of my reason and my will to steer a course that was good for me. Now, without realizing what was happening, my thoughts began to race beyond my ability to control them and to turn more and more inward. I paced the varnished wood floor, scarred from years of wear, and over throw rugs between wood-framed sofas and chairs while two dark-haired resident pooches made wide circles in one corner, like me, looking for some way to get comfortable. The pitch dark of the mountain night peered through the scenic windows, giving the place an eerie, disconcerting feeling. Dimmed lights stretched across the room from overhead hanging lamps, the only sound the clicking of the dogs' nails against the floor. I could not slow my thinking down. An hour or so later, I returned to our room. The cracking door woke Bill.

"Where have you been?"

"What do you mean, where have I been? I was out in the lobby."

Bill got up, looked me straight in the eyes, so close I could feel his breath on my face, and with the same angry whisper I heard from him earlier in the day, pointed to the bed. "Get into this bed, be quiet, and don't wake anyone up."

I lay in bed, my back to my husband, searching the dark for a sleep I couldn't find. I drifted in and out of a stampede of thought until the children woke like roosters to a new day. That evening we ate dinner at Jimmy's, a family restaurant in Lake Placid. Bill paid the check. In the parking lot he asked me how much money we had left. I told him we were down to only a few dollars.

He looked at me, baffled. "What do you mean? What have you done with all the money?" Bill threw his hands in the air. "You know we're supposed to be seeing Tom and Cheryl on our way home."

"Well, you know . . ." I looked him in the eyes so he could see the anger in mine, smoldering deep inside me, anger I was finding it harder and harder to douse. "Gift shops, souvenirs, things to remember our vacation by. I don't know. Things are expensive. You saw me buying them. Besides . . ." I looked over his shoulder, paying no particular attention to the entrance of the restaurant, "Bill, I just really can't go to Tom and Cheryl's. I haven't slept right since the kids and I left Ohio."

Bill walked me over to a phone booth between the parking lot and the road and crammed both of us in while our kids played in the parking lot.

"Call them and tell them."

I did not sleep that night, but lying awake in bed, I felt a kind of peace come over me. I didn't want to sleep. In fact, I felt ecstatic, a sense of what love must be like untouched by human limitation. I wanted to know more. As my family slept, I set myself against a pillow on the toilet seat in the bathroom and read from a book I had brought along: *The Four Loves* by C. S. Lewis. Time seemed to stand still as I read. I felt the sense of God's presence, as though He had drawn me to this time and place in the middle of the night, to a time and place where nothing could disturb me. Two or three times, I set the book down and slipped through the bathroom door. By the sliver of light behind me, casting an aura like moonlight on my sleeping family, I could see only my love for them. Three or four hours passed before I finally slipped through what was left of the dark, back into bed, and finally to sleep.

The next day, August 7, we left very early in the morning and drove straight home. We pulled into the driveway around 12:30 in the afternoon. Bill fed the children lunch and unpacked the car.

CHAPTER 15

FREE-FALLING

"My wife is sick," Bill whispered to a nurse.

We had been back from our trip only a couple of days when I found myself steered into the emergency room of Strong Memorial Hospital. Scared and thoroughly confused, I couldn't understand why he had brought me here.

"What time is it?" I pestered Bill. "What day is it?"

He kept assuring me that I was safe and needed help. I nagged him with questions, but I ignored anything he said.

The six o'clock news came on the TV in the waiting room.

"Do you hear them?" I grabbed Bill's arm. "The newsmen are speaking to me. Do you hear them? They're trying to take my kids. They want my kids."

An emergency room doctor walked over and introduced himself. "Hello, I am Dr. Lyman Wynne, chief of staff for the Psychiatry Department. Dr. Ruef gave me some of the details. Can you tell me what is happening?" He appeared distant and aloof. About six feet tall with thinning white hair, he bent his shoulders, stroked his beard, and lowered his head.

Bill tried to fill him in. Apparently, immediately after we arrived home, I had locked all the doors and windows, grabbed the kids, and hugged them to me, screaming, "Someone from the Mafia is breaking into our house!"

"She couldn't see the fear in the children's eyes, but I could," Bill told the doctor. "They're three, five, seven, and were terrified. I grabbed them and tried to calm her down. Joann was completely out of control. I called a babysitter, then Dr. John Ruef, who had been our family doctor for nine years. He told me to bring her right in."

He went on to say that during the whole car ride, I had kept shouting at the top of my lungs, "Somebody will hurt our kids! The Mafia wants to steal our kids."

Dr. Wynne had not looked concerned. He seemed more interested in writing down his evaluation than in how I actually felt. His admission papers were meticulous:

> *Thirty-three-year-old white female began accelerating four days ago, fearful and tense. She became increasingly paranoid, with fears of Mafia, and house being bombed. She thought she was bleeding on several occasions during interview. Needs observation in hospital setting where can feel safe.*

Does he really understand how I feel? Does he really understand what is going on in my head? I am angry. I am angry with Bill, I'm angry with Dr. Wynne, and in fact, I'm angry at the whole situation. Dear God, I think I'm angry with You. Should I be? I don't really have an answer. You made me to know, and love, and serve You. How can I do it in this condition?

"I'm so broken!" I shouted into the air. "Are You playing a bad joke on me?"

No, no, You are all loving and good. You can't do anything evil. It must be me. I burst into uncontrollable laughter. I couldn't stop laughing. I had lost all control of my behavior. An orderly arrived to escort me to a floor. I suddenly realized what was happening.

"Are you serious?" I shouted again and again. "Are you going to leave me here? Who will take care of my children?"

Everyone stared.

Within an hour, Bill admitted me under New York State's mental health law to the R-Wing, the psychiatric wing of the hospital. He scrawled on the admittance form, "Joann needs a lot of help to change her present condition." Someone handed me a form: NOTICE OF STATUS AND RIGHTS — INVOLUNTARY ADMISSION.

"What am I supposed to do with this?" I screamed at Bill. "There's nothing wrong with me! Someone is trying to hurt our children. I'm worried for the kids. My phone is bugged and the Mafia put a bomb on the porch."

A nurse came into the room and tried to give me some

medicine. "I'm not taking any medication. I think I'm pregnant." I shouted to anyone who would listen. "I'm worried for my children."

I grabbed Bill's arms. He took my hand. I yanked it away. He said he loved me, tried to console me. I ignored him.

Bill sank his head into his hands. He glanced out into the hall. He looked at me, told me he loved me, tried to soothe me with his words. But my thoughts were free-falling, grain by grain, from the rational world.

"I'm so afraid. Will you take care of our kids all by yourself?"

Bill said something. I couldn't focus on anything he said. He stayed with me another hour.

"Please don't leave. I am your wife," I kept repeating. "How can you leave?"

A nurse entered my room and tried to explain why I was there, something about disorganized, delusional, and disoriented. I insisted that I didn't need to be here but I would stay if I had to, to protect my husband and children and — I laughed out loud — to protect my country. The nurse asked Bill to leave. He was crying as he walked through the door. As he closed the door behind him, he looked through the window and continued to sob.

I felt so alone. I was here against my will. *Will he leave me in here forever? I'm terrified he will.*

Mary, a nurse, walked into my room and tried to give me some medication. I spit it out of my mouth. She noted on the psychiatric nursing admission form that I was disorganized and delusional. I denied any problems, but my chart reported recent difficulty sleeping.

I ate and fell into an exhaustive stupor for two hours. A nurse escorted me down to the lounge where patients were playing bingo. I could not focus on the game. Eight or nine people were in the lounge. I tried to make eye contact with some of them, wandering from table to table, laughing hysterically between stops as I introduced myself to anyone or everyone.

"Hi, I'm Joann." Some smiled politely. Others got up and walked away.

A nurse returned me to my room. I had not slept in any

meaningful way for three days. I collapsed into sleep until morning.

On August 8, Dr. Wynne, the attending psychiatrist, noted the following:

> *Joann is a thirty-three-year-old, married, from Rochester, admitted due to possible bipolar illness. Patient's condition has blown to psychiatric proportions. Has great tension and difficulty in organizing thoughts. Occasionally responds to unseen person's voice. Tends to hallucinations. Palms cold and damp.*

I do not remember this. There is no reason for the attending nurse to invent what she wrote. Apparently I danced down the hall, arriving at the nurses' station with my clothes off, rattling on in conversation with no one, tenuous—in short, borderline insanity. The nurse escorted me back to my room and helped me get dressed. I tried to read but couldn't concentrate. I paced the floor but could not get anywhere. I had a hard time staying still. I refused any medication.

Later, in the afternoon, a nurse took me to the lounge. I became increasingly more agitated. I could feel the tide of euphoria rising that I could do anything. I refused to talk with the staff and put my hands over my ears. I demanded to be released from the hospital.

Finally Bill arrived. All I remember is his walking into the lounge. His hairline was receding but he was still handsome, with the same warmth and kindness that drew me to him in college. I tried to look into his beautiful brown eyes but could not sit still long enough to do so. He put his hand on my shoulder. I no longer responded to gentleness. I ignored him. I jerked away and paced the floor. I snatched a ping-pong paddle from another patient who was playing a game, because I could. I flirted overtly with male patients, throwing mocking glances in Bill's direction as I did. Bill left.

Sue took me by the arm and started me down the hall toward

my room. I did not want to be alone, but distance from others seemed to be the only relief from my acting out uncontrollably. I thought about Bill. *I think I respected him very much. Why doesn't he respect me? Did the nurse tell him about my behavior?*

As much as some part of me wanted to cry out to him to rescue me from this hell, I couldn't. I resented his presence. I resented his sanity. After he left, I noticed my wedding and engagement rings weren't on my hand. Did he take them?

Mania, for me, had been elation out of control, an ascent through thought and a rush of emotion to the indisputable pinnacle of invincibility. I tried to sleep that night. I could not manage any more than naps. My existence encompassed a growing disdain for those of lesser intellect: nurses, doctors, and husbands. I napped, paced the floor. I napped, wandered the halls. I napped, and each time I woke, I climbed nearer and nearer to the pinnacle.

The following morning I was running through the hallway, yelling. A commotion erupted. Staff were ushering a man into a room and locking him down. I had never seen anyone placed in seclusion before. Afraid they might do it to me, I became more defiant. I ran to the piano in the lounge and began banging on the keys. By 6:15 a.m., Dr. Wynne had ordered me into seclusion.

Two nurses met me as I bounced back down the hall. I ran in the other direction, slapping my hands against my thighs and kicking my feet. The nurses took me by the arms, shuttled me into a dimly lit room, steered me to a mattress on the floor — the only piece of furniture in the room — locked the door, and left. One window with iron bars on both sides of the glass looked out to the sky. It looked and felt like a jail cell.

"God, why, why, oh why is all this happening?" I pounded my fists on the door, the windows, and the walls of the room, screaming and demanding to get out. I pounded and I screamed until I could pound and scream no more. I collapsed in a heap on the mattress, exhausted. I thought of my children, my babies, so sorry that all of this was happening. "When you say your prayers tonight, ask Jesus to help Mommy get better. She misses you very much but right now she is very, very sick."

Outside, the clinical, antiseptic world of medicine clamored along tile floors and painted walls, echoing wails of delusion or small talk, uncontrollable laughter or tears, the measured beat of doctors and nurses and orderlies plying their trade, all pockmarked by a brief spell of a strange, eerie, and foreign silence.

CHAPTER 16

THE BATTLE FOR MY BEING

Over the following days and nights, I groped for the sanity I could not find, swept in a flowing labyrinth of utter darkness. Dragged by a torrent of thoughts without connection, dredging emotion from the dregs of my soul, the whole stinking deluge of shame and guilt and self-contempt was driven by one primordial instinct: utter terror.

Angry with my husband for daring to be sane, desperate to protect my children from phantom enemies, I could not even begin to comprehend what my illness was doing to them.

And at that point I couldn't care. Exhaustion was my only friend. I would sit in a corner on the floor then jump up and pound the door because I could not sit still. I would squat down once more, repeat the same thing over again, collapse on the mattress into a comatose sleep, and, as soon as my body recovered enough energy, leap from the mattress, pound on the walls, scream, crumple to the floor in tears, forsaken by a mind ripped from my control, running like a hysterical child from the arms that would save it from itself. And all I could do in this misery was watch, as fear begot what fear dreaded.

No matter what I did, time would not move. How I wanted it to move: move forward to be through with this, move back to before all this happened, just *move* to get me out of seclusion and out of this prison. No matter how or where I put myself, it was no more than a fruitless attempt to make time pass. I lost all awareness of mechanical time. Whatever I had called life until now, every ounce of my strength battled the *now*, the battle for my being.

A phantom day stalked the window to the outside world. Beyond that window, the world sailed on in its enthusiastic indifference, with its lust for life, its infatuation with death, with my home, my husband, and my children. I lay exhausted in a hospital gown, cast adrift in a gray lifeboat, beneath a thick gray sky, on an endless gray sea.

If hysteria had cut loose the anchors of my sanity, the loneliness was breaking my heart. Nurses arrived at scheduled times to administer meds, but I was not allowed visitors. The door was locked, and my only company was the mattress on the floor. I don't know what light within blind-black dark means, but in hindsight, it is the only way I can describe the longing I felt for human contact beneath the rubble of psychosis.

A dull smudge of light grew brighter as morning approached. Outside my door, footsteps and voices swelled with the approaching light. With a rattle of keys and a crack of the door handle, a pair of arms slid a meal tray over next to my bed, and I ate. I have no recollection of what was on the tray, only that I ate and ate fast. As I ate, I looked down and saw bright red blood seeping into the towel I had been provided. I turned and saw the bloodstained sheets on my mattress on the floor. I had my period.

I jumped to my feet and began dancing on the mattress like a little girl, as happy as the little girl who used to dance for Papa Domenico back in Italy. I would have been only too happy to be pregnant again, though not being pregnant meant that I could allow myself to take the drugs that might get me out of this hell. Suddenly, as if someone had pulled me eye to eye and barked "Listen!," I heard birds singing somewhere, singing free somewhere out in the open air. I ran over to my window.

"I have my period!" I screamed through the closed window. "And all I have is this towel!" I folded it over and over. "The blood . . . it's bright red!"

The nurses' reports from the previous evening while I was in restraints made it clear that menses had begun. It had not registered. I was yelling and cursing at anyone who came near me, screaming that some mysterious *they* were trying to kill my baby. The staff had seen to my hygiene until I was placed in seclusion, when I adamantly refused any protection. Staff had come in frequently to change the bedding and give me another towel. I remember nothing but desperation.

I cannot say enough for the staff, how they tried in every conceivable way to steer me through this debacle of uncontrollable instinct. I have to rely on their notes to even begin to piece together what I was going through.

Shortly after breakfast, a nurse opened the door to my room and left it open, an attempt to see if I could manage a less structured treatment. I dashed out of the room, clung to other patients, could not handle any structure, and resisted returning to seclusion. Persuaded back to my room, I began to hallucinate. Suspicious of everyone around me, I pounded on the door, the walls, and the screens over the windows. Nurses made scheduled visits to administer Haldol to calm me down, which also stiffened the muscles in my arms and legs for some time after the shot. The Haldol spread through my body and left me gyrating around the room with my arms stretched out in front of me like a sleepwalking jester.

Dr. Wynne visited twice to look for signs of progress. A clinical psychologist on his staff also stopped by. Wait was all they could do. At times during the day, a nurse would enter to spend some time one on one with me in order to calm me down. I did not routinely make a run for the door as soon as it opened. At one point in the afternoon, I felt as if I couldn't breathe. I dropped to the mattress, staring into the ceiling vents. When a nurse arrived to help, I grabbed her so tightly that another nurse had to come to get my hands off her arms. By 4:30 p.m. I was again screaming and pounding on the door. When two nurses entered to make checks, I bolted through the door as they left and had to be physically invited to return. A nurse gave me Haldol. I spit the dose out of my mouth. Staff administered two more doses by injection that evening. According to the records, I fell asleep around 8:00 p.m. and slept through the night. The nurses checked on me every fifteen minutes.

The next morning, August 11, Dr. Wynne visited, finding some hope in the fact that I had slept through the night without needing additional medication. Waking up, however, was all that my mind needed for the salvos to begin flying again. He ordered more Haldol, which I took by mouth, noting that I was beginning to respond to careful nursing structure but was still "wary, guarded, and hyperactive." Once I had calmed down and the flexing and contortion of my limbs subsided, a nurse escorted me from my room for a stroll down the hall. Dazed but compliant, I returned to seclusion with little resistance and remained somewhat calm until midafternoon, when I began slamming my fists on the door. A nurse appeared with Haldol. I refused the oral dose. She countered with an injection. Once the muscle contractions subsided, I dropped to the mattress and fell asleep.

Exhaustion brought sleep. Sleep brought relief. Awake, the broadsides raged on. What was left of me endured in a hospital gown: paranoid, distrustful, unpredictable, clinging to whoever might come near me. Forgetful of staff and doctors and whatever they may have said, I slept until a nurse woke me around 9:00 p.m. to attempt a stroll down the hall. As soon as I cleared the door, I bolted to the TV room. Staff nabbed me before I could reach a chair and steered me back into the hall. On my way back to solitary, I overtook a short, middle-aged woman. I turned and hugged her. I clung to her and had to be physically separated from her, so desperate was I for human contact. Bill had been calling to find out how I was doing. He needed a lot of reassurance of progress, but I was never told of his calls. Any conscious thought of my family — my husband, my soul mate; my children, flesh of my flesh — had vanished.

The terrible, miserable, oxymoronic irony of it all was that I could not tolerate the very closeness I craved: the touch of another human being to satiate the emptiness in the cavernous depths of my existence. I could not handle anything but seclusion. This time, I took by mouth the meds brought to me by the nurse. I slept through until 6:30 the following morning, when I woke up and immediately began pounding on the door, ringing the call bell, and demanding to be let out of the room.

I have no choice but to rely on the records of Dr. Wynne and the nurses' reports for the next day. If there is any recall on my part of the events of August 12, they are lost to history. Dr. Wynne noted that I was finally quiet and, for the first time, clear and explicit about auditory hallucinations I had been experiencing and responding to but denying since admission. Up to the time of his visit, I could not distinguish between ward sounds and voices and hallucinations. I heard my mother's voice in my ears, reassuring me, and that of a childhood friend. I told the doctor that I had been hearing voices since childhood — a point Dr. Wynne noted as unreliable, and which in fact was fiction on my part. I forgot even the names of the staff I had just been introduced to. My ability to focus attention was still severely impaired — I was still fearful, but less panicky.

I remained relatively quiet until the nurses entered for seclusion checks. I would make run for the door, bolt past staff into the hallway and plant my feet into the floor, refusing to move, requiring two staff members to persuade me back into the room. I could not process information — there was too much of it flying around inside my head. At times I would try to orient myself to the outside world, emotionally unresponsive except for inappropriate smiling and an undertone of anger, suspicion, and distrust toward the staff.

And there was I, somewhere in the middle of three and a half days of seclusion, lost between two worlds, unable to grasp which was real, unsure of where the borders were marking one from the other. Yet if this was insanity, if all I could see or feel was darkness, something inside of me somehow still *knew* that a light existed. Some thread of faith tethered me to a sanity that now, in my state of desertion, seemed no more than a forsaken hope.

Have you ever read a book, set it back on a bookshelf, and moved on to the next book, and the next chore, until months, perhaps years later, some power grabs your consciousness and will not let go, pulling you back to a line in that book? You look up the line and realize that it has been trying to tell you something all along and you just didn't get it until now. In very much the same way, looking back through a generation of time, I sense what could not make sense to me then. When I saw the light of day appearing through the window of my seclusion, somewhere something inside of me knew that it was light, and that the light was beyond me, in a rational world.

And still I had no sense of time. I tried keeping track of days by counting sunsets — I could not do it. Yet somewhere inside of me, I knew that time was passing. When Dr. Wynne visited me and ordered a dose of Haldol by mouth, I obediently complied, only to throw a fit and spit the meds out when a nurse entered my room and tried to do the same thing. Somewhere inside of me, I still knew the sway of the scepter of authority. Through the smoke and haze of the inner turmoil I could at times, even if only for a sentence or two, manage rational conversation.

Within, the battle raged on. At times the tide ebbed. The thunder of the guns echoed somewhere off in the distance: a sudden jolt of fear, or a desire to fight off the recurring thought of being locked away forever. I paced, pounded, screamed through my solitary. Then time would flow in, bringing with it the mania. Invincible, I could do anything. I communicated with God. I pictured myself as President, a piano virtuoso, a best-selling author, an all-wise counselor able to bestow rectitude and wisdom on others to help them make a better life for themselves.

Dr. Wynne opted to gradually increase the dosage of Haldol.

Isolated, I was generally quiet and slept between checks, smiled appropriately, appeared unable to process what was said, with no irritability or manipulation until I was taken for a walk to the dining room around 10:00 p.m., when both traits returned. I was coaxed back to seclusion. The evening nurse noted that while in the dining room, I wrote my name and address and that my husband loved me. I vaguely remember writing in the darkened dining room. I have no idea how. Once isolated, I calmed down and became less manipulative and suspicious. I slept through the night, between the fifteen-minute checks of life in seclusion.

The following morning, the resident psychologist stopped by to assess my joyless enthusiasm. Around 9:00 a.m., a nurse escorted me to the dining room for a late breakfast, a new experience, for I had eaten virtually all of my meals in my room. There were only two other patients in the area. When they came to say hello, I could not sit still. The fear and distrust returned.

Yet, in the midst of chaos, what is strange is the silence. When the earth shudders beneath the feet of a village; when a wildfire charges through a forest with disdain for everything in its path; when explosions shred the customs of a wedding or a town square, the silence that follows bears witness to the deepest truth. Without any particular awareness on my part, the guns of opposing forces within me warring over control of my mind began to silence. I don't know how to explain this. When I was admitted to the hospital on the evening of August 7, I deduced that I must be sick, tried to convince myself repeatedly throughout this stay that I was sick. But the bone and marrow of my will to live had insisted all along that there was nothing wrong with me, that I was perfectly healthy and rational, that the doctors, the nurses, the hospital, just had it wrong. I could not realize that some conflict was beginning to heal, because I could not admit to myself that anything was wrong.

Around 1:00 p.m., after the dining room would have emptied, a nurse entered my room and asked me if I would like to go to lunch. She escorted me to the dining room. We sat together. I was slowly becoming less antagonistic toward, and more reliant on, the nursing staff. I ate moderately, carried on a somewhat rational conversation with her: no pressured speech, good humor, and only occasionally searching for words or losing my train of thought.

As we were about to leave the dining area, the nurse asked me if I would like to take a shower. I was delighted with the prospect. I had not had a shower since I came into the hospital. She took me by the hand and walked me down the hall and guided me to a shower in a room with a bed on a frame. I took a shower, washed my hair, and returned to the room, where my suitcase now rested on the nightstand. I dressed, found a book with my clothes, sat down on a wooden chair, and began reading with the door to my room open, as if I had stopped by Midtown Plaza for a cup of coffee, as if nothing out of the ordinary was going on.

Midafternoon, I walked to the dining room by myself and sat alone listening to a soft music radio station, wandering through a daze of Haldol, semi-exhausted and descending from somewhere as mysteriously and mystically as dew through dark, an intense sense of relief. After some time I felt enough confidence to venture into the TV room. I sat and watched television for a couple of hours, neither troubling nor being troubled by others, with only a few excursions down the hall. The only hint I could glean that anything had changed in my life was the encouragement from the nurses as to how well I was doing.

Mom used to find out if a cake had baked all the way through by taking a toothpick and poking the center as it neared the end of its time in the oven. If the toothpick came out with any batter on it, the cake needed more time in the oven. When it came out clean, the cake was done. On the afternoon of August 13, 1981, one of the nurses mentioned that my husband had called every day asking about my progress. I remembered that I had a husband and told her that I hoped to see him soon. Bill received permission to visit me for the first time since August 7.

CHAPTER 17

THE GREATER PAIN

A question wanders in the back of my conscious thought, like the lilt of a cardinal from deep in the woods. *Who bears the greater pain in a moment of crisis: the one suffering, or the ones seeing the suffering, utterly incapable of doing anything about it?*

By the time our family returned from Lake Placid in 1981, I had become like a paranoid, uncontrollable child. Since that afternoon, Bill had taken me to our doctor and to a hospital emergency department, and he had resigned himself to admitting me involuntarily to a psychiatric unit. He visited me that day, enduring my scorn, and also arranged for the care of our children, kept working, and called the hospital at least once a day, pelted by worry and fear over what would become of me as he stood at the helm of our life, his face to the wind, taking it all.

It may have been a nurse visiting me during the afternoon of August 13, 1981, who told me that Bill was going to visit later in the day. I do not remember. At that point I did not remember how long it had been since I had last seen him. I looked forward to seeing him but, like a crash of thunder after a bolt of lightning, worry echoed through the hope.

I tried to fix myself up. I dressed in a pair of slacks and a blouse, grabbed my brush, and went in the bathroom to brush my hair. I looked at myself in the mirror. Oh my God. I stared into the face of a woman exhausted from drug-induced sleep, with the strain and the stunned confusion of battle seeping through every line in her face. I still could not grasp what I had been through. Bill. What would he think of me? How would I react when I saw him? Would he still love me? What was going to happen? How would all of this affect the kids? Could our lives ever be the same?

I fidgeted. I walked the hall, walked to the lounge, chatted with whomever would talk, frequented the nurses' station to check the time. I finally went to my room, sat down at the desk, and waited. My back was toward the door. Whatever I was doing, I could not concentrate, listening instead for the sound of those footsteps I knew so well. Bill was coming to visit.

I could feel the presence of someone entering the room. I caught the flash of white from the corner of my eye as a nurse sat down on the edge of my bed and folded her hands in her lap.

"Joann, your husband is here." She reached over and put a hand on my shoulder. The nurse walked me to the lounge. I saw Bill standing about five feet in front of me. The fear and confusion on his face reflected my soul.

These are Bill's words recounting that day:

I do not know how many days had passed since being allowed to see Joann during the time that she was going through her breakdown. The staff encouraged me to call the nurses' station for updates on how she was doing, which I did daily. I finally received permission to visit. I was nervous and anxious, to say the least. What do I say to her when I see her? Do I hold her? Do I kiss her? The last time I saw her she looked so small, and confused, and scared. As I drove to the hospital, my mind was spinning around a whirlpool of unknowns, with no idea whatsoever as to what to expect.

I got off the elevator and fought the twenty or so steps across the waiting area to a door with no handle on my side. It shocked me to think that this heavy door was the only way in and out of the ward. I looked through a window the size of a paper grocery bag, looking for Joann. She was nowhere in sight. I pushed a button I found in the door, and a buzzer released the lock, allowing me to enter. The jar of that buzzer through the intensity I felt at that moment was like saying "Draw" in a gunfight. A nurse met me at the door and led me to the lounge, explaining along the way that Joann was in her room — better, but not well. I should just try to roll with the moment and meet her wherever she might be in any given minute and not expect too much too soon.

I saw my wife for the first time in a week. A very faint smile kept getting lost in a dazed, expressionless sorrow. Her eyes seemed to be saying, "I'm sorry," and deep in those eyes I could find no more than a thimble of the woman I had know for eleven years. I don't remember hugging her, nor kissing her. I might have touched her gently on the arm or shoulder as I left. She was very stiff in her movements and felt distant and agitated. We spoke very little during our half-hour visit, neither of us knowing where to look or what to say. As I left and walked back to the car, I knew that I had confirmed rather than soothed my fears. Would she get better? How long would her rehab take? What do I tell the kids about how their mother is doing? What will the next day bring?

After Bill's visit, I became more conscious of the state of my family and how this was affecting them. My head cleared somewhat. Some scattered but tangible sense of relief had punctured the clouds from above, and for the first time, I managed to carry on a conversation that I would remember. Later in the evening, I related to a nurse visiting in my room that I had lost track of my thinking when our family visited the mountains, and that I still felt a direct connection between the beginning of this episode and my fall in 1968.

A resident visited the next morning, gave me a passing grade to keep me out of seclusion, and allowed me to talk with Bill by phone. The first light of normalcy crept into view when staff returned furniture to my room. I would still get lost putting thoughts together but managed to pull them back into something resembling rational, coherent conversation. Bill spent some time during the day visiting with me. I reached the point where I could tolerate the presence of others and volleys of brief phrases with Bill without the rancor of the recent past.

I spoke with the evening nurse about my family, not being able to sleep for several days before admission, and my confusion over why I was "locked up" in seclusion. Beneath my apparent progress, a part of me still fought the notion that anything was wrong with me. The battle for my mind may have subsided, but the war was not over. The nurse noticed my fully packed suitcase and mentioned it. In her report she wrote what I said in quotes: "I don't plan on being here for long."

Bipolar slipped into the crevices of my consciousness as a crafty affliction, convincing me at times of my invulnerability, at others dragging my reasoning into sheer desperation for survival. It bears another crafty characteristic. In either extreme, I am confident of the accuracy of my own self-diagnosis.

On the morning of August 15, I felt clearheaded enough to hold a conversation with my nurse. I told her of my desire to go home but admitted to her that I knew I needed to remain in the hospital for the time being. I felt stiff and kept crossing my leg. I didn't like the side effect of the medication making me sleepy all the time but overall had a very good morning.

After lunch I slept until my 2:00 p.m. meds. Then I was paranoid, barking at my nurse, more than once saying, "You're like my mother. It's always, *You need to take this, you need to take that."* Galled that my husband was home with the family, apparently having a good time, while I was stuck in the hospital.

By 3:00 p.m. I was on the phone with Bill, hounding him to get me out of the hospital. I became extremely irritable, demanding that the staff discharge me. A couple of hours later, Bill visited and I settled down, made no more mention of going home, ate dinner, and spent the evening in the dining room hooking a rug bearing the image of a sailboat, a project I had begun and shelved years before.

So it would go for the next ten days. At times, the clouds thinned and the blues of high heaven scraped through with sunlight; at others, the clouds and fog rolled in and with them the terror of getting lost or sinking.

During the following day, I helped geriatric patients with their meals, simply because I wanted to, played ping-pong with another, and worked on my rug. I saw a copy of the *Democrat and Chronicle* on a chair in the lounge and noticed the date, August 16. For the first time in ten days, I had rediscovered *when*. Life again had a pulse, and I could feel it, I knew it, and I was elated.

Later in the afternoon, Bill and my sister slipped into the lounge from behind me. Lucy nudged the chair, grabbed me with a hug, and said, "Jo, you look great." I longed for familiar faces and felt a bolt of delight at the sight of hers. She handed me a large poster that she and my children had drawn and colored: a large brown squirrel carrying a load of nuts with the caption, "We're nuts about you."

It hurt, but I didn't let it show. I wondered why she brought me a poster that seemed to be making fun of my plight. She was probably trying to make me laugh. Did my sister understand? How could she? I didn't understand myself.

I drew a smile from the depths of my will to live and suddenly realized how much I missed my children, so grateful that they remembered me, so plagued by what they might be thinking of me, aground on an illness I still denied, unable to reach them and care for them. The three of us traded small talk for twenty minutes or so, at the time my limit for staying focused.

Around 5:00 p.m. a new nurse visited for a one on one. I gave her some of the details of my circumstances. I had tried doing too much while on vacation in the Adirondacks with my family, which led to my going out of control. I had taught chemistry and other sciences ten years before but stopped teaching in order to raise a family and was happy doing so; I just wanted to get back to them. I tried to cast a pleasant façade. I denied any problems other than that I tended to push myself too hard.

Later in the evening, Bill and my mother visited. She and my sister had arrived from Ohio to help with the family a couple of days after I entered the hospital. Given the history of tense moments with my mother, the medical staff had thought it best to delay the visit. By this time I wanted my mother to visit, and she did.

I don't remember if I asked Bill about my father. I don't remember what room I met my mother in. I don't remember the features of the unit I had been confined in for over a week. I vaguely remembered enduring a war over my sanity, one flashing instant firing into the next for days on end, with brief truces when I could look out and understand that a world beyond my own existed. When I saw Mom that evening, she was that world. Looking at her, seeing her face, I tried to read how she was going to take this. The woman who taught me how to cook, how to sew, how to clean the house—I felt as though I had let her down again. I was ashamed of what she would think of me. Somewhere deep inside of me, longing to be loved by her for whom I am; somewhere deep inside, fearing what she was thinking.

Bill put his arms around me and smiled, then stepped aside. I looked my mother in the eyes as I took a few steps to where she was standing. A trace of a smile on her lips spanned the silence. I gave her a polite hug. Bill sat down in order to give us some space.

She hugged me. "Do you want me to be here?"

Exhausted, hoping to get well enough to go home, I didn't want to risk a serious conversation. "Mom, I'm glad you came."

"You wouldn't be here now if they took better care of you when you were in college."

"Mom, my accident wasn't their fault. I'm the one who fell. I didn't tell anyone."

I remember the anger in her voice blaming all of this on the fall in 1968 and the six-month aftermath, grateful that Bill was in the room. She aimed her anger away from me. I felt a sense of relief that she cursed what had happened rather than blaming me, but her lecturing over my past wrung the hope from my still-uncertain future. Her ire ebbed by the time they were ready to leave, and she embraced me with genuine concern. Perhaps she accepted the fact that it was no one's fault.

"How's Dad?"

She told me that he was getting better but hated the hospital.

"I'm praying for you . . ." She looked me in the eyes and, for one brief, flickering instant, in her eyes I glimpsed the realm within her known to her alone. "We have to trust in God that you'll get better."

Bill gave me a kiss as he hugged me. "Hang in there."

They walked away in silence. Bill turned once and nodded.

Mother had come from Ohio without my father and would need to get back to him. Dad had remained in Ohio, hospitalized once again with chronic gout and severely ill from a drug reaction. I felt helpless enough, confined in a hospital, knowing that others had to carry my weight. I needed to know why my father had not come, wishing I did not know once I found out.

I grew up with his condition and saw how he suffered through it. I wanted to go visit him, keenly aware of what he must be enduring. Yet all I could do was stretch out through this longing to be with him and hold his loneliness in mine.

When I was twelve years old, Dad began tossing math questions at me, the way boys would play catch with their dads in the backyard. He enjoyed testing my skills; I enjoyed the challenge. I don't remember my father telling me he loved me. It was something we learned over time, something we just knew. Throughout my life he routinely encouraged me, telling me of his pride in my intelligence, my ability to learn, and my accomplishments as a student. The tenderness he showed me. These were the simple gifts of everyday love I remember him by, the love by which I will always know him.

CHAPTER 18

RECOVERY AND RELAPSE

Dr. Wynne had told me that I suffered from bipolar disorder caused by a chemical imbalance that exists within the pathways of the brain, causing a loss of ability to relate thoughts in a clear and coherent manner. By August 17, 1981, the medications were suppressing the bombardments of disjointed thoughts, allowing me to think more clearly. I managed a superficial display of pleasant cheerfulness, which helped me to believe that I was recovering, though it did little to convince the medical team. Though my health was returning, beneath my portrayal of contentment anger simmered. To the resident who visited in the morning, I blamed my admission on Bill, who had been angry with me for going through our vacation money in two days. To Dr. Wynne who visited later in the morning and to the nursing staff, I complained about my mother's visit the previous evening — "She's wonderful, but she's overbearing, treating me like a child" — feeling that in her presence I must always be on guard, very seldom able to be honest with her about my feelings. But I could not come face-to-face with my own anger.

Once more, time refused to yield. I longed to get home. I wanted out of the hospital, a discharge, a pass to go home, anything to put this behind me. After all, I was fine. The doctors scheduled a CT scan for the following week. I did not want to face another week away from home. Once more, guilt flowed through me like a returning tide, bringing with it the responsibilities I now knew others were bearing. Stephanie would enter second grade, Stacie would begin kindergarten, and someone needed to take care of Michael. I had chosen to stay home to take care of our children rather than work. Here, I was capable of neither. By the grace of God, Dr. Wynne agreed to let the children visit.

The news of a visit from my children filled the sky with light. For hours I announced the tidings from the nurses' station to the lounge, from the dining area to the precincts of our rooms. I tried to knit, I tried to hook the rug Bill brought up to keep me busy. I watched TV, visited friends I had made. Nothing worked. I could not concentrate on anything. Seeing my children became my greatest longing and most dreaded fear. We had always been physically affectionate as a family: hugging, kissing, laughing, crying, and expressing our love for each other as much by body language as by the rhythm and music of the words of everyday life. I never wanted to lose the homespun intimacy of this warmth. I feared the first look on their faces, the flash of lightning from their souls before they could remember how they were told to behave, the innocent, unfiltered reaction to my companions and me. How I dreaded that first glance. I couldn't bear to see pity in their eyes. Would they see me as different, as broken? I felt reasonably coherent and practiced my best behavior all afternoon, but I still suffered from the side effects of the medications, which left my limbs stiff and made it very difficult to sit still. I wanted so desperately for our lives to return to normal.

After supper, I set myself down in a beige striped easy chair in the lounge near the one doorway to the hallway and waited, listening for the sound of their voices. A half-dozen patients scattered through the lounge found some comfort in the drone of a television playing in a corner. My eyes danced from face to face, to the ping-pong table, the magazine rack, and the corners of the room. Whenever they came to rest, they rested on my hands and arms, which were stiff and extended out like broken arms without casts, a side effect of Haldol. What was I going to do? Who knows how many fragments of hell I had drawn up from the bowels of human existence and pounded, and fought, and cursed, and raged into a purgatory of desperation just days before? What would I say? How would I behave? Would I do or say something wrong? And the greatest fear of all: would they still need me?

I heard them before I saw them. I started crying. Until that moment, I never knew I could miss anyone so deeply. I cried in joy, I cried in despair. They were too young to understand — would I lose them in what I had been through? Stephanie skipped into the lounge followed by Stacie and Michael, all giggling with delight, utterly indifferent to their surroundings, the center of their lives focused on one human being. I had not seen them in ten days. Ten days of forever spilled through their eyes and filled the room with light. Bill stopped short, just inside the door, silent. Like three beautiful butterflies, Stephanie, Stacie, and Michael fluttered around me. Like a caterpillar transformed by the solitary isolation of a cocoon into a butterfly, I soared into their freedom. Small and delicate, they wrapped their love around me. I don't know how long their visit lasted. All I know is that their innocence endured my sense of failure. I felt the strength of their presence. Nothing to this point had given me such a feeling of recovery. Nothing to this point had given me more of a reason to live. We hugged and said goodbye. Their feet shuffled down the hall.

I felt like my world was leaving with them.

I sat mute in the lounge, deep in thought, unable to recognize myself, unsure of what I was feeling. I felt a profound sense of relief in the presence of my children, so grateful that to them I was still Mom, soothed by their falling all over me and, in their innocence, their inability to judge me as anyone other than the person they had always known. Their ease with the circumstances allowed me to fathom from this morass of confusion a purpose for being, beyond the mere will to survive. So strange that when I was admitted to the hospital I was convinced absolutely that I was perfectly healthy. Now I began to see how sick I had been and how I needed to get well for them, because they loved me without judging me. They could not feel my fear. They could not see the debris within me from the days of battle for my sanity.

Earlier in the day I had agreed to Dr. Wynne's request that I remain in the hospital until the CAT scan and EEG were completed the following week and to allow the staff time to adjust med doses and to discuss at length a workable discharge plan for my return home. Now I sat lost in my thoughts. Was it minutes, an hour? Time again had lost its significance until a nurse arrived, sat next to me, and asked how things were going. I spoke openly with her about my need to go home the following week in order to get the children ready for their return to school. I wanted passes to go home. After some time in the lounge, I returned to my room. That night, my illness paid another visit.

I had pinned my hopes on a return to normalcy, or what I called normalcy. A return to home life, my husband and children, the daily routine of our American dream—and denial. I wanted nothing more than release from the hospital, to put it all behind me. To pretend, as I did in 1968. But looking behind the mask of who I pretended to be, this was the terror of it all: in the end, how alone we really are.

The next day, the children returned, strolling down the hall behind Bill in the wake of the aroma of the hot pizza he was bringing for supper. And something amazing happened: the nurses allowed me to leave the unit in order to eat outside with my family. We found a picnic table beneath a huge shade tree on a stretch of lawn between the street and the hospital. If ever there was a remedy for confinement, it is a dose of freedom. For the first time in eleven days, I felt a breeze on my face. Sun speckled the grass through leaves lazing beneath an August sun. Mountainous patches of cumulus clouds, typical of late summer here, lugged in the waning days of summer. Utter joy surged through the thrill of watching Stephanie, Stacie, and Michael bounding across the grass just like pups released from a kennel. I could taste the illusion of freedom, taste it like chocolate on my lips: the illusion that I could leave with my family and go home, the illusion that this was the reality, that the real illusion was *there*, within the walls of the hospital. And for a brief span of this brief day of temperate fear, a tide of contentment that I could not hold back flooded in over the rubble of this August, and for one brief visit, the guilt that tortured me slipped beneath the tide and disappeared.

Patients who were well enough lined up each day at the nurses' station for their medications. The following day, I took my place in line. When I appeared at the counter, the nurse handed me my pills, but not the customary cup of water. I stood motionless, not quite sure what to do.

The nurse smiled and nodded over my shoulder. "The drinking fountain is behind you."

For the first time since my admittance into the hospital, I could actually do something for myself.

I made friends during my three-week stay: transient friendships that brought much relief but remained confined to that time and place. A terrible sense of loneliness appeared in my life with the arrival of bipolar. I craved conversation. It's difficult to think of friendship with nurses and doctors, given the rapport required by their profession, but I can think of no other word to describe the relationship during my stay. The nurses were tough when they needed to be, tender when tenderness was all one human being could offer to another in the throes of distress, but always compassionate, even as it was, so often, in the midst of mayhem.

The sojourn outside with my family allowed me a taste of liberty and, with it, a yen for the creature comforts of daily life. I had smoked cigarettes since my college days only occasionally and socially, except in my experiences of deep duress. I had not smoked for several months but suddenly found myself longing for the taste of a cigarette. At that time, patients could still smoke in hospitals. I watched others enjoying the habit and recalled how much I enjoyed it. That day I *really* wanted a cigarette. For those who have never smoked, it must seem perverse; for those who have, who know how wonderful the taste of tobacco can be, it must seem miraculous. I asked a nurse for a cigarette. I pleaded with her not to tell my husband, not that I had smoked, but that I had asked someone for a cigarette; he did not like me bumming them. With the wave of a hand, she gestured not to worry and handed me what happened to be my favorite brand. I relished smoking every puff of it.

A sense of friendship on the unit brought a sense of comfort that we, orphaned by our right minds, still held a connection to the world of the sane and rational. I spent time with a soft-spoken frail elderly lady with short curly gray hair, helping her with her meals at times, at other times talking with her, simply because I had always enjoyed speaking with older people. Our conversations, like most on the unit, were more in the nature of shared monologues than dialogues. We were both here because of our inability to deal rationally with the outside world, but the act of communicating nourished the need to believe in our selfhood. At times I was still adrift in the lifeboat, tossed about by a confused sea, trying to ride the waves and tame life once again into some kind of manageable habit. I could not see my illness as part of myself but as an infection or the wayward drift of some part of my body, which could be corrected and the problem ended. Communication, no matter how trivial, helped to feed the illusion that bipolar and I were strangers crossing courses, going to blows, and each of us heading off in different directions.

One of the great elixirs of trivial conversation during the closing days of my confinement was the courageous duo of a spare-haired, heavy-smoking, lean chess player and a tall, muscular, heavy-smoking, and smooth-faced gentleman who looked like he was from the Wild West. We wandered the unit together or sat in the lounge and smoked cigarettes. After I received hospital privileges, we roamed the halls together. The one who wore a cowboy hat seemed to have diplomatic immunity, allowing him, it seemed, to enter and leave our secure unit at will. He bought us cigarettes and never questioned why we needed to smoke. The trips into mindless chatter after the mental confusion of just a week before were sheer delight. They helped me to regain a sense of identity and self-worth more than Bill or anyone else did. This was because they did not dread and fear my illness.

On Wednesday, August 19, Dr. Wynne reduced the dosage of Haldol. Bill and I met with him and the treatment team to discuss the treatment plan through the end of my hospital stay and after my discharge. They clearly defined the nature of my disorder, its gravity, the possibility of recurrent episodes, and the need for a gradual return to normal activities. They agreed to a series of trial passes over the following days: dinner on Friday, a four-hour pass on Saturday, and a longer pass on Sunday. Dr. Wynne's treatment plan was to reduce and eliminate the Haldol, gradually replacing it with lithium and planning discharge when my lithium levels were adequate.

After Bill left, I joined my pals for dinner and weightless conversation, eventually settling into the ten-by-twelve-foot world I called home since my release from seclusion six days before. As I idly thumbed though a magazine, the full impact of our discussion began to press into my thoughts like yeast through bread dough. What did Dr. Wynne mean by lithium prescription? Did he mean that I would have to remain on medication, as in, *there is no cure for what ails me*? My hopes were to leave all of this behind. Somewhere deep inside of me I could feel the opening of the abyss from my days in seclusion haunting my prospects, the timeless fear of an incurable condition that would cripple my ability to reason.

The passes to leave the hospital felt like a reprieve and a major step toward recovery. At the same time, I felt like a school child needing permission to do anything. I presumed that the medications prescribed during my stay in the hospital, like a prescription of antibiotics, would run their course and I would be healed. In order to be discharged, I agreed to all of Dr. Whynne's stipulations, yet through all of this, I still maintained that there was nothing wrong with me. I had been admitted for exhaustion, and once I was no longer exhausted, I would no longer be sick. Now, the thought of needing lithium indefinitely made me wonder if I had undergone some fundamental irreversible change that would leave me vulnerable forever.

The next few days leading up to my discharge led me down paths in directions that seemed to contradict each other. I watched pieces of my life changing color. Still unsure of who I was or how well or sick I might be, feelings pulled me one way, then pushed me another. The hospital had created a sense of security and structure. I wanted to be released but feared the liberty of responsibility for making decisions again. I had consented to a diagnosis that deep down I denied. Yet I was an involuntary patient, and the stigma would leave its mark.

I continued to walk with rigid limbs and outstretched arms. I dreaded the possibility that the side effects of medication might never completely subside. One-on-one conversations with nurses revolved around recurring themes, which I clearly needed to come to terms with if I was ever to find the peace of mind that eluded me. I cried when I talked about my father, probably because he was not with me through this due to his own illness, but I think it touched something much deeper. I remembered how much I missed him when he left for America when I was four. I sensed that I never really healed from the pain of that separation.

I had been raised in a strict household, which meant that I learned to obey. In learning to obey, I often forfeited my right to feel my own feelings. I carried this into my adulthood, often finding it difficult to say no. Under so many circumstances I found it very difficult to express how I really saw things, leaving a trail of smoldering resentment that I was being imposed on by others.

At times I still struggled with saying no to my mother. It had become clear to the staff over the course of my stay that being more assertive with her would be one of the requirements for discharge to go home.

The passes granted gave me a sense of hope that soon I would be free, but I still felt a tide of anxiety pulling me out of the depths of an unknowable future. Uneasiness in the presence of others, especially if they approached me, lingered on. I began to realize the importance of being alone—then the terror struck. I needed time to feel the comfort of being alone, but was this a trap? Was this the disorder, drawing me into the isolation I dreaded? When I looked back, for a moment all that I could see were instances of feeling alone under a suffering from which I could not escape.

Bill arrived by himself on Thursday to accompany me on the first of my three passes: a two-hour release into the free world. I heard the door of the unit lock behind us, fanning the embers of an excitement I feared as we walked to the elevators. Hand in hand we strolled through the doors at the entrance of the hospital, as if we were on a date. The fresh breeze of a sultry August evening tried to wash away the rush-hour stains from the city air. The cemetery across the road reminded me that life still pulsed through these veins, giving life to these eyes. As we drove away from the hospital, the world seemed the same on the outside. The world rolled on, blithely disinterested in the specifics of any particular life. We went to get something to eat, I don't remember where.

Yet I didn't know what to feel, how to feel. Bill and I ate and talked as if the world had disappeared, but when he took me to a store to buy some shoes, I felt the world inside closing in. I became more and more self-conscious. Like the first light an hour before sunrise during the long days of summer, I could feel a deep sense of joy, of excitement, the promise of light somewhere out beyond the horizon. Yet it was as if darkness prevailed, still trying to swallow the light—the inevitability of returning to the hospital, lingering doubts about my own recovery, and, worst of all, the dawning realization that my feelings were still in seclusion and had been right all along. I had two glorious hours to breathe free, but free under the scepter of authority within me. Obedience. I was lost amidst my emotions, never sure of what I would be allowed to feel, unless I received the permission of another.

Two days later, Bill arrived with Stacie and Michael to escort me out on a second, longer pass for four hours. My mother and sister had returned to Ohio with Stephanie in order to take some of the pressure off of Bill. We went out for dinner and stopped at home briefly afterward. I enjoyed being a family—at least I told myself as much. Stephanie, my little helper, was in Ohio. I grew restless as the children fidgeted and fussed and bounced around, enjoying themselves. I felt isolated in the presence of my family, unsure of myself. I found myself looking to Bill for visual clues as to how to behave at any given moment. I knew I had to concede that I really could not handle another baby at this point of my life.

I toured my own house, trying to get my bearings once again, to see if I instinctively knew where everything was. I needed to try walking the stairs. In the basement, manicured sheaves of sorted laundry bore the imprimatur of my mother's visit.

Deep among the pillars of my soul, I could not escape the dread of having to confront my mother before I could leave the hospital. Once again the agony of divided loyalties, trying to find a way to please everyone, tinted every hope gray. We returned to the hospital early. Everyone said goodbye at the door to the unit. I meandered back to my room through my own disappointment. It began to occur to me that I had thought I was healthier than I really was.

CHAPTER 19

RISE AND FALL

When I crossed the Atlantic Ocean to America with my mother and sister, I was so excited by the adventure, so enchanted by such good fortune. It was as if an angel woke up each new day and spread heaven before my eyes. After our first meal on the *Andrea Doria*, as we strolled the main deck, we heard a long blast of the ship's horn. Mother said that the ship was getting ready to leave. It was not until some time later, when we heard three long bursts from the horn, that the ship began to move, lugged by tugboats out into open water. The mighty steam engines surged to life, pulsing through every fiber of the ship. This city of the sea began to move, slowly gathering speed as it slipped between the islands Ischia and Capri. Naples faded into the horizon as the *Andrea Doria* settled into the sway of the sea. Soon all that lay before us was the vast Mediterranean and the adventure of what was to come. Our life lived in the mountains and our family still fresh in my mind, it was as if all I had to do was flip back the pages of a storybook and there they would be.

My love of school and learning absorbed my new life in a new country. The visits my sister and I made next door to drink soda and eat chips at the Angelonis' before the saloon opened were a thrill I looked forward to each day — where I learned English before I even started school. Disappointment reared from time to time through my years of growing up, but an impression of joy prevailed and bound to my determination. This my faith and upbringing taught me, and I learned my lesson well. Perhaps too well. As I grew, I learned to think about my feelings instead of feeling them. Over time I mastered the ability to suppress emotions, along with any spark of spontaneity that accompanied them. Only in hindsight did I begin to realize the paradox in this.

For three weeks I struggled for my sanity through scouring storms of terror, desperation, and animal instinct to survive. I could feel these emotions to the core of my being. The feeling I could experience the most was fear: fear of failing in my responsibilities at home, fear of relapse and the return to this.

My third pass, for six hours, allowed me a longer visit home, a chance to try to construct some sense of normalcy, a return to daily routine. I returned to the hospital a bit early, repeating to nurses over and over throughout the evening how grateful I was to have such a caring and supportive family. Eventually, one of the nurses sat down and told me that it was all right to admit to myself that being around family could be stressful at times.

Though I knew in some rational sense that I was getting better, whether in the hospital or out on a pass, at times I could feel my anxiety rising. I could hear my speech racing. As the days to my discharge drew down, I became more anxious: excited to go home but fearful I would not be able to handle children and a household. I still fought the battle of superficiality: showing the nurses how pleasant and cooperative I could be while at the same time troubled by the deception, knowing that the staff knew, and knew that I knew, that I was not being honest with myself. Deep in my heart I still believed the illusion of my own making that there was really nothing wrong with me other than being exhausted and stretched too thin.

I had asked for permission for Lucy to visit on the morning of August 24 to say goodbye before her return to Ohio

She did not stay long, as she had a long drive ahead of her, but she gave me hope: something positive that, with a new prescription, seemed to be uniting my feelings and my thoughts once again to the same plane of existence.

That morning I began a prescription of lithium carbonate, gradually increasing the dosage as the dose of Haldol was lowered. Lithium induced fewer side effects and would be the long-term treatment for my disorder. For the next couple of days, until my discharge on August 26, I melted into the population of the unit, hoping to become invisible to the staff, leaving nothing more than a trace of my visit. I hurried through the halls, socializing when necessary, intent on hooking a rug in my room or in the lounge when I could, the clock ticking off the hours. I bided my time. Occasionally, my thoughts would begin to race. At times, fear, the puffing viper, rose and coiled between the future and me. I did not trouble the doctor with questions about my discharge or the course of my meds. I assumed that he would take care of these details. The nurses encouraged me to be more involved in my own course of treatment, but I expected to be freed from this illness, not bound to it.

I was discharged almost three weeks after my admittance and left the hospital with my husband, my suitcase, discharge instructions, and a medication that offered hope for a future of psychological equilibrium. This was the day I had been waiting for. I looked for ways to sense what I thought was supposed to be a resurrection to health: take the medicine, take it easy, take a sabbatical from the pressure of family, and all would be well. But I still felt as though I had a cloud hanging over my head. I was depressed. The trust I held in others had survived this ordeal, but my trust in myself had been leveled. Being instructed for weeks to listen to the direction of others because my own judgment had failed reinforced my upbringing that I could really only trust the voice of authority. I had convinced myself that I was not worthy of respect from anyone. My self-esteem continued to deteriorate. I shared these thoughts with no one except for my husband. I carried this dark secret that I suffered from bipolar disorder. I dreaded that people would find out. I did not discuss the intensity of this fear with Dr. Wynne. I kept it inside. And it ate away at me.

The first week home, Bill and I met with Dr. Wynne three times. Bill drove me to Dr. Wynne's office located inside Strong Memorial Hospital. We arrived and entered the main door to the lobby. I became obsessed with the terror that someone would recognize me and wanted to put a brown paper bag over my head. Like a thief in the night, praying that no one knew me, I followed the red lines along what seemed miles of corridors, almost collapsing with relief when I made it safely to the elevator.

"Come in, come in." Dr. Wynne's secretary sat behind her desk, her long black hair falling across her face as she leaned over her schedule. She nodded toward the inner office. "Dr. Wynne is expecting you."

I had not *imagined* the jolt of shame that struck when a lightning glance from the secretary revealed that my fear was obvious. No matter how I tried, something inside of me knew that I could not conceal my secret in Dr. Wynne's office. I scuffed through the door; my limbs were still under the influence of the remnants of Haldol.

The doctor smiled as he rose from a dark green upholstered chair, extended his arm, and directed me to a chair opposite him, next to Bill. I slouched into the chair, either with an air of resignation or an air of exhaustion, facing the doctor who brought me back from oblivion, the doctor I had come to esteem with near reverence.

I listened much and spoke little, depending on Bill to explain how I felt, literally aching for an end to this affliction. Dr. Wynne seemed to take it all in stride, arranging for blood work, discussing further treatment and the course of medication with us, a ritual we would practice weekly, then monthly, as my condition improved, a relationship between me and medication that would continue for many years. Serious and devoted to his field, Dr. Wynne always remained relaxed and easygoing.

"Doctor," I asked, still trying to tame the occasional involuntary bobbles of my limbs. "All I want to know is when will all of this end?" This was a question I would press home with him over and over throughout the course of treatment.

"Joann, you have sustained heavy doses of Haldol, which are constraining. We are gradually eliminating this medication and replacing it with lithium carbonate. The muscle spasms will subside and disappear over time. We have to take this step by step."

Over the course of months, I began to shed side effects and adjust to a sense of normalcy, but I had failed to fathom how long the journey would be. I did my best to listen to every word Dr. Wynne spoke, but I had to listen over and over again, appointment after appointment, before I could begin to absorb what he was telling me. Across the span of several years, we fought the battle for my peace of mind. Only in hindsight could I begin to comprehend the significance of my condition. I had become my own worst enemy, playing to whatever audience I had to perform for. I listened to what Dr. Wynne said, I did what I was told to do, but somewhere in the core of my being dwelt an adversary, convincing me that I was truly healthy. I just had to play this game. Without my being aware of it, this stubbornness of denial affected virtually every decision of any relevance that I made—and herein lay the dread. Was the disease of bipolar disorder laced through the ingredients of my personality, or was this a stubborn, hardheaded resistance that I always possessed?

Bill had arranged for a babysitter to care for the children so he could return to work. The discharge meeting at the hospital required me to agree to rest and to gradually return to running the house on my return home. A family friend suggested a sweet, middle-aged woman whose children were grown to come and help with Stephanie, Stacie, and Michael. I had wanted my arrival home to confirm my ability to rule, but my children were under the care of another, and I had no choice but to submit.

I had come to this point of my life, in part at least, because I could not admit to myself that anything was wrong with me. In short, I would not allow myself to be sick. I had to be sunk and hurled into a lifeboat, stripped of my ability to control, and steered to a conditional surrender. I had to concede that I could not physically endure all of my duties. I spent hours each day in bed, still battling depression and the road trip of side effects from the medications. When the children were home, I forced myself to cheer up and feign an air of normalcy; I did the same if a visitor arrived or someone came to the door. The mania of my hospital days had collapsed into the abyss of depression at the opposite pole of bipolar. When the performances ended, I would fall into bed, exhausted.

The babysitter talked and played with my children while I endured upstairs, resting or sleeping, the dawdling pace of the step by step that Dr. Wynne had foreseen. She fixed them breakfast, lunch, and snacks for several weeks. One day, I decided to walk downstairs and into the kitchen during lunch and noticed small peanut butter and jelly sandwiches on white bread. Mine would have been larger and on whole wheat bread. It wasn't the sandwiches that bothered me, but my jealousy. I wanted my life back. I prayed for the day that I could return to taking care of my children.

I forced myself to do more. By the end of September, I was sleeping better and lost most of the restricted motor activity that had characterized my functioning prior to the reduction of Haldol. My fine motor skills still suffered and I had trouble reading and writing, but I could drive in the neighborhood and take care of my children with help, at least part of the time. By the middle of October, we decided to try to move on without the babysitter, to let me try to run a home again.

Life moved on, as life must. Slowly, with the help of lithium, I recovered. We, as a family — how do I describe this — almost imperceptively set out to recover what we had always believed to be a normal family life. I think Bill and I wanted to believe that we could simply erase the events of August 1981 and live on as if it had never happened. In the depth of my illness I could not relate to anyone in any meaningful way, but I never stopped loving my children. I instinctively wanted to care for them. But I never discussed my illness with them, never really came face-to-face with what this event might be doing to them or Bill. My illness became the elephant in the room that no one wanted to mention.

In the months following my discharge from the hospital, my appointments with Dr. Wynne were reduced from weekly to monthly. I continued to get stronger and was still under the impression that lithium would cure my illness.

The path back to normal life appeared straight enough, but I walked the path on two feet, each it seemed landing steps in two different realms: one in my outer life, one in my soul. Looking out on the world, I could sense progress. Although I tired easily and needed to rest more often, I was able to manage our children and take care of our home. Little by little I graduated from simple meals to full dinners. Sunday evenings we resumed our tradition of salad, cheese, and *pizza fritta* (fried dough). Like sweet summer rains cool and quench a thirsty evening, I could feel relief in the simplest tasks. My first trip driving the car went no further than the corner deli, but the sense of freedom elated me. To sense agility in my limbs, to be able to set a table or cook without dropping a plate or a utensil, to be able to write again, felt like a return from exile.

Looking inward, however, watching the steps walking my soul, I held my doubt. Days would come along when I could not function. Bill would have to stay home and take care of the kids. One day, perhaps late October, a neighbor knocked at the front door and I answered. I saw the look on her face as she asked me if I would help with a church project. Like the first time Bill came to see me in the hospital, the look on her face showed me what I could not see in myself. I told her I had been in the hospital and was not up to the task. She returned the next day with a large basket of homemade cookies.

Lightning glimpses in the eyes of others — relatives, neighbors, friends, acquaintances, and especially Bill and the children — revealed for no more than an instant the raw, unrefined fear or concern stalking their courtesy. This would shred my confidence. Hospitalization, therapy, counseling, medication were teaching me how to live once again, how to shape the guilt of this ordeal into a manageable process of reason. The glimpses from the eyes of others struck a deeper world, exposing the bedrock of shame in me, the stigma that could not be reasoned away, because it had burned into my soul. And this, I feared, had become who I was.

So often I willed myself to heal, determined to put this all behind me. So often I had to fall once again. Depression dragged me to a halt and threw me into bed, held me down, and would not let me move. I spun off to the limits of my endurance, and somewhere beyond the reaches of those limits, someone was trying to tell me to slow down the marathon and wake up to the instants, the moments, the nows that I had been ignoring. While I battled what I had been and what had occurred, what I needed to do and what needed to be done, I was blind to the very life that enabled me to do it. I was buried somewhere beneath this rush to fulfill, this rush to heal. This rush to please. I lost the holidays of 1981. I remember nothing of the days with my family, other than the vague recollection that we spent them alone.

As 1982 entered the world, I could feel the lithium knitting my consciousness into a pattern of thought and feeling that I could begin to comprehend. But the swings between extremes continued, and I still did not know which was going to win.

CHAPTER 20

MY FATHER'S LAST VISIT

My father came to visit for a week in February 1982, despite my mother's objections. They rode from Canton to Rochester by bus. The kids and I picked them up at the bus station in downtown Rochester on a cold and snowy afternoon. I drove home and we entered through the side door. The first thing my father did, still in his coat, was go to the refrigerator for a beer. I always had beer on hand for his visits, but this time I had been so busy I forgot all about it. I offered to go to the local deli and get him a six-pack.

"He doesn't need any beer," my mother interrupted.

I shot a long glance at my mother that made it clear I was buying the beer. I drove to the corner deli and returned ten minutes later, six-pack in hand. Dad heard me walk through the door from the garage into the kitchen where he sat at the table. He glanced at me, then the beer, and broke into the smile that had told me for as long as I could remember that he was proud of me.

I started supper. Dad drank his first bottle of beer, a perpetual creature comfort for him. God was once again in heaven and all was right with the world. My father never asked for much, and I knew it would set things right with him.

Dad thoroughly enjoyed his visit. His delight was playing with his grandchildren, and the delight radiated from him in their presence.

On the second of March, just a couple of weeks after my parents' return to Ohio, our phone rang around 10:00 p.m. My sister informed me that Dad had picked Mom up from work around 6:00 p.m., came home, and collapsed from a major heart attack. Dad was dead.

I was in shock.

Bill and I and the children left the following morning for the six-hour drive to Canton. A part of me couldn't wait to arrive. Another part of me — deep beneath the measured beat of time, where life keeps its secret fears — wished that I never would.

Our life together here had not been particularly easy or tranquil. The man who once dreamed of being a teacher labored in a clay pit. Later, when we moved into our first real house, he worked in a metalwork factory making airplane parts. These were times that we saw little of him during the week, but I knew he was coming home. I couldn't fathom what he went through emotionally in the war, but we could all feel the impact of his descent into those tortured memories. So often he could not contain the fury within him. So often it charged through the battered armor of his reason and fell on us with merciless indifference. Then calm would return. He would laugh and joke, praise and encourage, allow himself to love and be loved.

Only months before, in the psychiatric unit of the hospital, the part of me that held the pieces of my life together was losing to an unbridled, heartless instinct for survival. Days of isolation filled with hours of minutes that lasted eternities leached the meaning from my life, leaving nothing but a numb and homeless emptiness. Through weeks that followed, I was drugged, isolated, tied down, secluded, and counseled back to sanity.

Desperation or terror can drive the human spirit into the vast wilderness. There it comes face-to-face with how separate and alone it is, how vulnerable and finite life is. Dad — what had he been through? What made him the way he was? All that I knew of him on the trip home was that, in the core of my being, in this wilderness couched and waiting just outside all of the pretenses of civilization, a fire had burned day and night. A man had appeared long before, built the fire and tended it, provided a shelter and food in the wide, humble nowhere of humanity. The fire cooked our food, warmed us from the cold, and gave us light to scare away the dark. And at times, the fire could burn with fierce intensity. Through all the tranquility and torment, the labors and the love, the highs and the hells of my life, through it all, one man had tended this fire. Suddenly, the fire had gone out. I will be grateful to my dying day for the spark that leapt from that fire and stung me into fetching Dad's beer for him just a couple of weeks before.

A small brick church, reddish-pink in color, in a small Ohio town—St. Francis Xavier Church—remains the keepsake of my childhood. The entrance faces South Carrolton Street in Malvern. My sister, mother, and I attended midmorning Mass. Dad would regularly attend the early morning Mass. There I had received my First Communion and Confirmation.

We entered the church and seated ourselves in the front pew to the right of the altar. Many from the town attended the Mass. Most had known our family since our arrival from Italy. Lucy and Scottie, who twenty-six years before had been with us at the death of my sister Erminia, took their seats a couple of pews behind us. Father Victor, who knew Dad well, was the main celebrant at the Mass.

Words had flowed through mourners for three days, mantras of condolences to soften the blow of unexpected death. Today we faced saying goodbye, for the last time, to the head of our family. Beneath the words, the prayers and the eulogies, the tears, the silence of death waited for the interment of life in the church cemetery. Silence haunted the depths of mourning where love and need collided in a final kiss on a cold coffin.

Yet something occurred on the day of my father's funeral that I have wondered about ever since. Events come to pass in life that defy explanation. I can only describe this sensation as it happened then and feels to this day. At one point during Mass, I felt the depression lift from my life. It was as if Dad had stepped into the pew behind me, touched me on the shoulder, and said, "Jo, I've been freed of my pain. I can take some of yours for you."

PART THREE:
THE RISE

CHAPTER 21

HOW LONG WILL REMISSION LAST?

Several months passed after my father's death. They were filled with doctors' appointments and blood tests. I continued to get stronger and was still under the impression that lithium would cure my illness. There were still hypomanic days, but I was learning to cope with them.

On my appointment on February 23, 1982, Dr. Wynne related to me that I was in what could be called a full clinical remission. We officially reported that I was now functioning better than at any time in the past, including the years prior to my psychotic episode the previous August. Physically, Dr. Wynne said that I appeared extremely well and had no somatic symptoms.

Our lives were going so well that Bill and I decided to go on a ten-day trip to Myrtle Beach to celebrate our tenth wedding anniversary: June 10, 1982. We drove the children to Ohio first, then we were on our way. I sat next to Bill, the loving husband who stuck by me through the many peaks and valleys that someone with bipolar disorder goes through. It was a fun trip. I was truly in remission. I still had my mood swings, but they were subdued. Lithium took care of those. I was in remission for the rest of June and July.

I was doing so well that on August 9, 1982, Dr. Wynne started me on a trial off the lithium to see if I really needed to take it. I was all for it. A placebo was used and double-blind basis took place for nine weeks. This was an experimental procedure in which neither the subject nor the persons administering it knew the critical aspects of the experiment. He did this because I was totally free of symptoms or problems from bipolar disorder.

I was able to stay off of lithium for about a month and a half. He urged me to start taking my regular dosage again if I felt that I needed it. I would put myself back on it when I became sleepless, confused, and on the verge of a manic attack.

By September 1, I had been on a placebo for several weeks.

Dr. Wynne stated during this appointment: "Patient appears to be unchanged from her previous asymptomatic status."

At this time, Bill and I kept journals, noting anything else about the marriage or family life. We brought these journals to the meeting on October 18, 1982.

I had been on placebo for seven weeks. I was asked to participate in a placebo-lithium trial. I agreed to do so. In his report, Dr. Wynne states, "The double-blind trial took place for nine weeks." During the first sixteen days of this trial, as we learned after the October 18 interview, I was given active lithium unchanged from my prior dosage. I recorded on October 2 that my husband thought I was going in too many directions again, although I didn't feel that I was. After that date, I made no more journal entries, and at the same time Bill became more and more alarmed. He was describing me to Dr. Wynne as "hyper," "irritable," "very touchy," and "getting involved in too many outside activities."

On Friday, October 15, he tried to talk to me about slowing down. I simply became upset with him and started crying. He wrote: "This is the first time she's been this way in over a year." Finally, on the weekend before the October 18 appointment, I acknowledged that I was getting overcommitted. I tried, with some success, to do less.

Dr. Wynne wrote in his notes during that meeting: "I feel that she is mildly hypomanic and definitely different than she has been in the past year. There was a somewhat frayed quality about her. She appeared not only edgy but also quite tired of being edgy. She spoke about the fact that her thoughts kept racing and jumping from one thing to another so she had a hard time distinguishing anything. Subjectively, it appears that the pressure of the racing thoughts is the most distressing symptom she now has. She thought that she could keep things under control without returning to lithium, and we eventually agreed that she would have a three-week trial openly off the lithium. I suggested that we could evaluate. If Joann felt that she needed the lithium, she was encouraged to take it."

On Tuesday, October 19, 1982, in the middle of the night, I swallowed a lithium capsule, the first dose that I had taken in a couple of months. That capsule gave me the assurance of getting better.

Over the following years, I continued seeing Dr. Wynne and was taking the lithium, and I was in remission. I was living a relatively normal life. Periodically over the years, I would take a break from the lithium. Usually after a month or so, I would have to start taking it again. I was beginning to think that I would need to take it for the rest of my life. I had never asked him why he took me off of it once every few years for a month or longer. I think it was to see if I could be weaned off it and whether I might not need it completely.

CHAPTER 22

NEW BEGINNINGS

From the death of my father in 1982 to the late summer of 1989, I lived a "normal" life and faithfully took my lithium. To the best of my recollection, the placebo trial in 1985 was the last one we conducted until 1989. I was able to care for my husband and children, I volunteered at church and school, I visited with my friends, and I substituted in local junior high and high schools.

During the 1986–87 school year, I taught part time at Our Lady of Perpetual Help School in the city of Rochester. I taught seventh- and eighth-grade science—two classes a day, four days a week. During the interview for the job, I said I only wanted to teach four days a week because I had small children. The principal agreed and hired someone else to teach health on Wednesdays. She offered me the position and I accepted.

In January of 1988, a friend called me and asked if I wanted to teach earth science. One of the local Catholic high schools let a teacher go and needed a replacement. It was not my field, but I told her to drop the book off and I would take a look at it. I read the earth science book from cover to cover. The subject matter seemed easy enough. I accepted the position and began teaching right away, from January to June 1988.

I was offered a full-time teaching position for the 1988–89 school year, but I declined. I had already signed a contract to be the religious education coordinator at St. Thomas the Apostle Church. This was a part-time position and I could set my own hours. I only had to be in attendance on Sunday mornings and during special classes for First Penance, First Holy Communion, and Confirmation. This job sounded too good to be true.

Father Callan had interviewed me a couple of times in February for the position. He told me he appreciated the fact that I was a good Catholic and was confident that I would pass on the Catholic faith to our children. I respected him and knew that he would support me in our work together. I signed my contract on March 3, 1988, and began working on June 1.

I enjoyed the work a lot and summer quickly came to an end. The religious education classes began on the Sunday following Labor Day. They were conducted for an hour on Sunday mornings after the 9:30 a.m. Mass.

My entire family helped. Stephanie and Stacie unlocked all the doors. Michael turned on the classroom and bathroom lights. Bill supervised. I was stationed in the school office greeting the teachers, parents, and children. Classes ran through the end of May, but I would continue to work through the summer.

My first year as religious education coordinator was filled with successes. The families we served were thankful that their children were learning the Catholic faith. Our second graders received the sacraments of Penance and Holy Communion from the parish priest. Our eighth graders successfully received the sacrament of Confirmation from the bishop. We had plenty of adults who volunteered to teach in the program. My secretary, Thea, answered the phone, made copies, and fielded questions. She was like an angel watching over me, very religious and wise. Together we maintained a well-run program.

The year went quickly and before I knew it, it was over.

At the end of the school year in May 1989, Father Callan said to me: "Administration of all the sacraments has gone very smoothly and I'm very pleased with your work."

"Thank you," I replied. "I enjoyed it very much and this job has deepened my faith in God. It's this faith that sustains my life."

Stephanie was now fifteen years old and a sophomore in high school. Stacie was thirteen and in eighth grade. Michael was ten and in sixth grade. The events of 1981 seemed like a story in someone else's life. My life now revolved once more around my family and my involvement with church and school. I enjoyed attending PTA meetings, volunteering in the library at St. Thomas, attending the children's soccer games and piano recitals.

Bill had accepted my illness with equanimity but also with a deep sense of frustration. We had put it on the back burner. Bill and I only discussed my bipolar disorder in private and only when it was necessary. I was not sure this was the right approach in dealing with my illness, but Bill supported the choice.

"Look, you've been in remission except for the trials for almost eight years. I love you. We'll get through this."

The children didn't ask questions about my illness. Maybe we all wanted to believe, to hope, that the events of the past would be left there.

To the best of my recollection and my records, I had trials off lithium in 1982, 1984, 1985, and 1989. After each of the trials, I went back on the lithium and once again went back into remission. Dr. Wynne and I agreed to begin another trial off lithium on August 2, 1989. I was to take my last dose, 900 mg, and continue my hiatus until I felt that I needed the lithium again.

This method had always worked, and after each trial, I would resume taking the lithium. Remission and a normal life always followed. But that year was different. I was convinced that I didn't need the lithium, that I was okay. By the end of August, Bill grew very concerned about my behavior and begged me to resume taking it.

I met with Dr. Wynne again during the first week of September. He strongly urged me to start taking the lithium again.

He had been my doctor for nine years. I had trusted him. He had correctly diagnosed bipolar disorder. It was difficult to stop going to him, but my thinking wasn't clear and I thought I didn't need him anymore. I didn't see Dr. Wynne again until 1999 when I met with him and he gave me copies of my medical records.

During the months of August and September, my children and husband were alarmed at the way I was acting and kept asking, "Are you all right? Are you all right?"

In my mind I was not sick. "Of course I'm all right, can't you see that I am? I'm cooking dinner. Can't you see I need help?"

During the months of July, August, and September. I registered students and made plans for the approaching year. My office was located on the second floor of St. Thomas the

Apostle School and had windows on three sides with a door to the school. I felt very safe, peaceful, and comfortable there. I was in my own space and could not have been happier.

The calendar said Thursday, August 10, 1989. I was in my office busily working, but I would have loved to smoke a cigarette. I had an unopened pack of Merit Lights and matches in my purse and all I needed was an ashtray.

Looking around, I spotted a glass candy jar with a variety of hard candies in it on a shelf. I unscrewed the lid and used the lid for an ashtray.

I felt no remorse when I lit the cigarette and sat down to work. There was a NO SMOKING sign in the building. *No one would ever know*. I cracked one of the windows, put the makeshift ashtray on my desk away from all my papers, and savored this most-wanted cigarette.

The following Thursday, I was in my office smoking another cigarette, deep in thought, trying to decide if we should get new textbooks for the seventh and eighth grade classes, when I heard the locked entry door into the school open. It had to be someone who had a key. The stairs creaked. Step by step, someone was walking up to my office. They knocked on my door, turned the knob, and entered.

"Father Callan, how nice to see you." I put out my cigarette. I was sitting at my desk, but he was much taller than I was and towered above me.

"Joann, some parishioners have reported to me and to the principal that last week smoke was coming from your office window and they said that you were smoking a cigarette. Is that true?"

"Yes."

"Now I see that you are smoking again. You know that it is unacceptable behavior, as well as against the law. What is happening to you?"

I must not have given him a satisfactory answer because later that morning he telephoned Bill and asked to meet with him.

"Joann has been exhibiting some strange behaviors that are

not acceptable. She was smoking in her office." Then he asked, out of the blue, "By any chance does Joann suffer from bipolar disorder?" Father Callan had served as chaplain at the Rochester Psychiatric Center for at least twenty years before becoming pastor at St. Thomas the Apostle Church. He was familiar with mental illness.

Bill conceded, "Yes, she does. She was diagnosed in 1981."

Father answered, "That explains her behavior. Please take care of her. She is receiving medical help?"

Bill answered, "She is under the care of Dr. Lyman Wynne."

Father Callan said, "You and your children will probably have to take over most of her religious education duties, but let her do as much as she can."

Bill agreed.

Bill was very concerned and expressed his frustration to me later. "What's going on, Joann?"

"Why is he complaining?" I asked Bill. "All I'm doing is smoking a couple of Merits. There's no school. No one else is present. I'm doing God's work and don't think *He* minds."

But after that day, I no longer smoked cigarettes in my office.

"How do you feel?" Bill asked one day while we were alone.

"I'm okay, but I am beginning to have trouble sleeping." I resented the question. At the same time I wanted him to hold me, tell me we were okay. I told him I wanted to leave the house right then and there and run up the street.

He tried to talk me out of leaving the house. I waited about thirty minutes then ran to the corner of our street and St. Paul Boulevard to have a cigarette.

It was late morning. I stopped on the way to chat with my friend. She asked me with a concerned look on her face if I was feeling okay. She was a smoker and understood how I felt. When I reached the corner, the traffic was pretty heavy, but I didn't care. I sat down on the sidewalk and lit a cigarette. I inhaled, then exhaled, watched the smoke rise into the air, and felt a sigh of relief. I needed some physical distance from home to put things in some kind of perspective. I thought about Bill, and then

Stephanie, Stacie, and Michael, and how my behavior affected them. My eyes wandered down St. Paul Boulevard as I stared deep into my own soul. Then I thought about God.

I was taught the Catholic Faith, the catechism faith, how we are to live our lives; that we are to know, love, and serve You in this world and be happy with You in the next; but the catechism doesn't say anything about bipolar disorder or mental illness. When I was young, I wanted to serve you as a doctor, go to Africa and cure the world of its diseases; but my head injury when I was twenty-one put an end to that. My love of science still led me to teaching, but now I'm the one who needs a cure. I don't understand why I have this illness . . . Is this Your will? Is this how you want me to serve You?

I crushed out the cigarette.

I know You are in charge of my life . . . but why did You give me such a difficult one? Did You think I could handle it? You gave me a submissive acceptance of affliction . . . on the surface I am leading a normal life . . . well, I'm trying my best but some days my best isn't good enough. Some days I come apart and then my family suffers. Don't get me wrong. I have experienced many wonderful days and years, and for all of these I am truly grateful. Right now, I have no choice but to accept my life and the cross I have. I have persevered through all my sufferings and I have lovingly tried to take care of my family. What you spoke to St. Paul is the only consolation I can feel right now: "My grace is sufficient for you."

I looked at my watch and realized I had been at the corner for over an hour. I had to go home. Religious education classes would begin the next day, the second Sunday of the month, on September 10, 1989. I was there but secretly relied on Bill to tell me what to do. I smiled at everyone and camouflaged the turmoil that was in my soul. The next day, I asked my husband how he would feel about taking over my job.

Bill sighed. "Why won't you agree to go to the hospital? I feel really bad but am only trying to help you get better."

Sunday after classes, I walked home from St. Thomas ahead of my family to make brunch. I was dressed up in a navy suit, white blouse, and gold earrings. On the surface, I looked normal and put together. By now my husband and children, for all practical purposes, had taken over my duties at church.

A couple of weeks went by. Early in the afternoon of Friday, September 22, I was back at the corner of my street smoking the last cigarette out of the pack. I received some funny looks from many drivers. I waved to them as I sat cross-legged on the sidewalk. One older woman who was in a passing car waved her cigarette and smiled at me. I took my last puff.

Bill walked down to the end of Hermitage Road with Beth, my smoking buddy. They came to convince me that I needed to go to the emergency room. I didn't want to listen to them. I quickly got up and raced home. I had been at the corner for three hours. A couple of neighbors were mowing their lawns. I ignored them.

Bill followed me into the house. The three children were in the kitchen. He gently explained to them, "Your mother is not feeling very well and needs to go to the hospital." I overheard every word he said. I knew he was right.

Bill packed me an overnight bag, leaving fifteen-year-old Stephanie in charge so he could take me to the emergency room. She knew I was not well.

Bill helped me into the car. I thought of Thoreau: "Most men live lives of quiet desperation . . ." Hidden beneath a smile and a fully composed disposition was a woman in turmoil. Bill drove me to the hospital. On the way, he said, "You haven't taken your lithium in over a month and you are in the middle of another manic attack."

"No, this is not manic. This attack is different."

I didn't want to admit it, but at times I was having feelings of grandeur. What I was experiencing was not like the attack I had in 1981. At that time I experienced full-fledged delusions and hallucinations. I was completely out of reality. The ones that were occurring now were different and milder. I was more in touch with reality than before.

We continued to argue about what my fate would be.

"I want to be home for Michael's eleventh birthday."

Bill ignored me.

Outside the emergency room at the hospital, I yelled at Bill, "Give me the car keys, I want to go home. And it's too far to walk and now it's raining."

Bill tried to walk me through the emergency room entrance. I pushed him away, jumped up onto a concrete retaining wall, and started running. I managed not to fall off. I stopped running, sat down on the wall, and lit up another cigarette.

"Get down," Bill cried out. "Why are you smoking again?"

I stood up as if I was going to jump. "What am I doing here?" I was delirious at this point.

"Get down," he begged.

I took my last puff and then jumped. I landed on my feet, sat down on the pavement and lit up another cigarette. This was my last one. I crushed the pack up as tight as I could and threw it on the ground. It was getting dark.

"Will you buy me another pack, please?"

I was running back and forth outside the emergency entrance of the hospital. "Please don't make me go in."

We walked into and out of the hospital, repeating this scenario over and over during the next couple of hours. We continued to argue. I went back to walking on top of the cement wall. Bill stayed with me but I ignored him. *Should I go home or be admitted?* I walked, then ran, and then sat down and had a cigarette. He gave me another pack.

I paced back and forth in front of Bill. "What do you mean, I have to go in now? There's nothing wrong with me."

Bill tried to explain to me what the medical personnel inside had concluded. "You are in what is called a hypomanic phase. You have a distinct period of elevated, expansive, or irritable moods, decreased need for sleep, are very talkative, and at times have an inflated self-esteem." He took his Yankees baseball cap off and whacked it against his leg.

I didn't want to discuss this anymore. I turned and walked away from him. "I don't really want to be admitted; you are putting pressure on me to do so."

I sat on the sidewalk, smoking another cigarette. Bill called a social worker out to see me and how I was acting. The social worker did not think I should be admitted. Bill then told him that I stopped taking my lithium about five weeks ago and that I was on the verge of a relapse. The social worker finally agreed to admit me for observation.

I was involuntarily admitted as an emergency admission to the psychiatric ward on September 22, three days before Michael's birthday.

In the emergency room, I said hello to a good-looking older lady and a young man who was there with a broken foot. I was escorted to a draped cubicle. I sat on the examining table and waited. A couple of people finally came in. After my examination, a doctor and a nurse evaluated me. They agreed that I suffered from bipolar disorder. I was admitted as an involuntary mental patient around 7:00 p.m.

I pulled open the drape to the next examining room and peeked inside. A man wearing only long, red plaid pajama bottoms was sitting down. He told me that his name was Randy and that he was in for drinking way too much. He looked like my father.

The nurses assigned me a room and Bill helped me to get settled. He was anxious to get home to tell our children what was going on. He was very, very quiet. He left at 7:45 p.m.

I was alone. Anxious, I wondered what I should do. I didn't have any of my earthly belongings with me. *Where are my pajamas? Will I sleep in my clothes?*

One of the nurses, Nancy, brought the small overnight bag Bill had packed with my clothes, pajamas, toothbrush, and toothpaste. I sat on the cushioned wooden chair next to my twin bed. I thought of my family and how alone I really felt. There were no pictures on the walls. Suddenly my room grew smaller and I felt those walls closing in around me. I walked out of my room and wandered down the hall and approached the nurses' station. A heavyset nurse with wavy black hair and dimples leaned on the counter.

"May I help you?"

"What the hell am I doing here?"

"We're just trying to help you. Is there anything you want?"

I returned to my room.

About fifteen minutes later, the same nurse came in and asked, "Would you like to see a movie? They are showing a comedy in one of the lounges."

"Sure."

Her name was Sylvia and she walked me down the hall to the lounge, a large room with an open doorway. It was well lit and there were about fifteen people watching the television. The only place I found to sit was a large sofa and there were already two people sitting there. They moved over and made room for me. Sylvia stood at the door. You could feel her presence in the room.

Several minutes later, a guy with straight black hair and a receding hairline, dressed in blue jeans and a black leather jacket, entered the room. He looked around and then sat next to me. Five minutes into the movie, he put his arm around my shoulder. I did not fight it at first. I was flattered by his attention. He helped me out of my depression for a brief moment. Sylvia walked over to the sofa and told him to move. His name was Tom. I thought of Bill and the kids again and pushed him away. The movie ended around 10:00 p.m.

The next morning, in the lobby area of our floor, Tom brought me a cup of hot black coffee. He introduced me to his friends Robert and John. Robert was slightly shorter than John, whose eyes danced through shocks of very dark brown and wavy hair. He was an anxious young man about the age of thirty and he always tapped his fingers on the back of his chair. Very cordial and interested in why I was here, John was debating if he was going to stay, since he admitted himself voluntarily the night before for excessive drinking. In other words he was drunk when he came in. He decided to stay. Tom appeared a little spacey but behind the outward appearance he was thoughtful and generous. He told me that he was leaving the hospital. He voluntarily admitted himself; he could voluntarily leave.

"Enjoy the coffee, and I hope to see you around."

I never saw him again.

His friends became my friends and their friendship sustained me through all of the pain that I experienced during the three weeks that I was once again an involuntary mental health patient. Robert and John were the daring duo, always teasing the nurses. I wondered as I watched their antics what they would do next. I never told them how much I appreciated their friendship, but I think that deep down in their hearts, they knew how much they meant to me.

The only other female in the group, Janice, was in her early twenties and showed a keen sensitivity toward the feelings of others, along with many talents, including those of an artist. My first impression was her beauty, her intense blue eyes, her long, straight blond hair, and her radiant smile. She played the piano, liked sports, and attracted others with a natural charm. If looks could talk, they'd say she was a clean-cut young lady who had the world at her fingertips. A couple of days after her admission, just the two of us were in the hallway when she touched my shoulder and looked me in the eyes.

"Can I talk to you?"

I asked her to walk with me. She told me that she was from out of state and had been admitted for a problem with drugs. She mentioned friends in Rochester, but not her family, and her desire to be a dress designer. I told her my mother was one. In time she asked for a recommendation to a community college, which I was happy to do. I wrote it on November 14, 1989, after I was discharged.

My first Sunday in the hospital, Jake and I attended a Catholic Mass together at 10:00 a.m. in the hospital chapel. "Here I am, before your presence, Lord, and with my new friend." I worshipped quietly but my friend Jake bellowed out the words of the hymns as loudly as he could, almost to the point of being a distraction to me. He devoutly received Holy Communion, as did I. I marveled at his enthusiasm.

Matt, another young man, was tall and thin, the most sensitive of those I met there. Matt shared his most profound thoughts with me as we walked through the halls. I mostly listened because I was not ready to share my thoughts. What I shared with my fellow patients was mostly day-to-day information of a general nature, unless a conversation took a spiritual turn. At this point, I felt as though my faith was the only strength left in me, and to find others searching their faith for answers brought me comfort. I asked the Holy Spirit to guide me and I was not afraid.

I had asked Bill to bring my rosary-making kit. I was making them at home in my spare time for the missions ever since a good friend of mine gave me the materials many years before. I had enough plastic beads, crucifixes, and thin white cord to make a hundred rosaries and had made them sporadically over the years. The rosaries were blessed and then sent to Catholic missions throughout the world. Making them here allowed me to reflect on my life and become more peaceful and closer to God.

Another member of the group was Stan. Short, athletic, with a pack of cigarettes rolled in the sleeve of his T-shirt, he wandered the hallways, his bright blue eyes devoid of emotion. He wrote notes to my husband asking for cigarettes and to make sure it was a pack of Winston 100s. He gave Bill the exact amount for each pack down to the penny. During our three weeks together on the unit, the only other request he made was for a brown rosary when he discovered that I was making them in the lounge.

Beginning on September 24, we were required to attend Mental Health Teaching by a nurse on the unit. Meetings were every morning. It reminded me of school, except that I wanted to be the teacher instead of the student.

"Today's topic is choices." The peppy young nurse smiled compassionately across the ten of us. She neatly printed the topics on a whiteboard:

WHERE YOU'RE AT, GET TO KNOW YOURSELF.

WHAT DO YOU FEEL LIKE?

SPENDER OR SAVER

I felt more at ease, more able to control my reasoning. I asked several questions. The nurse answered politely and clinically. But I thought, *Is this supposed to help me? I don't think so. What I need is divine intervention.*

The next day was Michael's birthday. I called to wish him a happy birthday before he left for school. I knew he would be eating breakfast. I felt as though I could be strong for him.

"Do you know when you're coming home?" He sounded concerned, but I sensed he was trying to put distance between himself and a situation out of his reach.

All I could say was, "I love you."

I felt helpless as I spoke with Michael. I fretted and felt down in the dumps most of the day. I felt cheated. I wanted to be with my son to help him celebrate.

Around 5:00, Bill, Stephanie, Stacie, and Michael walked into the lounge where I was sitting with my friends. I jumped up and ran to them, hugging Michael first.

"I can't believe you came!"

"I know how much you wanted to be with Michael today." Bill carried a pizza and a concerned smile. Stephanie held a birthday cake. Stacie followed with plates and napkins. We asked the handful of people in the lounge to join us. It was awkward, but Michael was happy, and for a brief moment I was happy. I was home.

After they left, my behavior went downhill. I was depressed and felt that my life was over. I refused some of the meds; I convinced myself I didn't need them. I yelled at nurses. I played loud music in my room. I skipped some of my meetings.

Several days later, I slept from onset of the afternoon shift till 2:45 a.m. I skipped to the nurses' station and walked away quickly. I was escorted back to my room. I began fussing with my personal belongings. I stretched out my legs on floor and put my head in my hands. I was given 5 mg of Haldol at 3:00 a.m. The nurse noted: "Patient shaking hands, spilled Haldol on floor. Another dose prepared for patient. Patient accepted medication. When she drank water, patient did not shake. Furniture removed from room to decrease stimuli. Personal property removed. Patient instructed to remain in room on mattress, which was on the floor." I heard the click of the door as it locked.

At 4:00 a.m., I was officially secluded for assertive language behavior. For the next thirty minutes, I looked out the room window and the door window while walking quietly in the room. I slept on the mattress for about an hour, awoke and sat up, then went back to sleep. According to the records, it must have been some time later.

> *Three staff and two security officers entered seclusion room. Patient in good control and cooperative with staff, able to follow directions. Patient given breakfast and gentle firm instruction regarding her behavior.*

My seclusion ended at 9:00 a.m. The rest of the day was normal. I had my evening meal in the dining room at 5:30 p.m. and behaved well.

Bill arrived for a visit around 6:45 p.m. I began talking loudly about a patient's rights to a good doctor, to refuse medications, or to sign myself out of hospital. Bill attempted to calm me down. That is all I remember.

Apparently I then turned and slapped Bill on the side of his face with an open hand. Three staff members removed me from the hall to my room. To this day, I have to read the medical report to believe it happened.

> *A complete explanation was given to Joann regarding the reasons why she was taken to her room, the meds to be given and the reasons for them and her lack of proper impulse control and judgment was pointed out. Patient was verbally abusive to staff. Patient secluded at 6:50 p.m. for verbally abusive/physically assaultive behavior. Patient monitored every five minutes during the first twenty minutes of seclusion time. She initially stood at the door, staring out the window in the door.*

Thereafter, she lay down on the mattress on the floor, covered by a sheet. Appeared to sleep in about fifteen minutes.

When I woke up, I knew where I was. I had no idea what time of day it was. I went to the nurses' station. One of the three nurses told me that it was six in the morning and to go back to my room, as I would not be able to go to the lounge until seven.

In the midst of all of this, I had not forgotten the faculty and staff of St. Thomas Religious Education. I called the office daily and offered my thoughts and ideas to everyone. They in return sent flowers, notes, and cards with their prayers for a speedy recovery. I was most grateful for their prayers. God had already worked many small miracles in my life.

Father Callan came to visit me several times a week and brought me Holy Communion. I considered Father Callan my spiritual director at this time. If he could believe in me, others could believe in me. I could begin to believe in myself again.

He would often stand next to me before he left, a priest with pensive blue-gray eyes and thinning gray hair, in command of his thoughts, and give me his blessing. "I talk with Bill and the kids almost every day. They're holding their own. You need to be strong, keep your faith, and trust in God."

During one of his visits, a very tall and anxious old man recognized him, followed him, and asked him for Communion. I don't know what Father said in his ear but he did not give the man the sacrament.

Later that day, I spoke to my new doctor. He asked me several questions about Bill, my children, and myself with sterile, clinical efficiency. I did not feel like answering them. I had been through this routine before and was tired of revealing my soul to strangers. I had to have a different doctor since I was in Rochester General Hospital. He spotted my organic chemistry textbook on the table and inquired why I had it. I didn't want to bare my soul. I told him I had been a chemistry major and was reviewing. I had no desire to tell him — and I don't know if I knew myself at the time—that years before I still held on to the dream of returning to teaching science. He smiled and left the room, but not before telling me that along with the lithium he had prescribed Ativan (for anxiety, withdrawal, depression, panic attacks, insomnia) and Thorazine (for schizophrenia and manic-depression), which changes the actions of chemicals in the human brain. Over the next few days, my temperament began to level off. I was grateful to be back on lithium.

First nurse's check each day was at 5:00 a.m. I fell back asleep. When I woke again, it was still dark. I turned on the light. I didn't know what time it was but I knew that I was looking forward to my first cigarette of the day. I had to wait until 7:00 a.m. I should have gone out to see what time it was but I wanted to do more writing first. I had been keeping a journal for at least fifteen years, a paragraph or two a day, even as I slipped away from normalcy. I don't know why, but I thought of the words to "The Battle Hymn of the Republic" and decided to write them down. I sang to myself as I wrote:

> Mine eyes have seen the glory of the coming of the Lord.
> He is trampling out the vintage where the grapes of wrath are stored.
> He has loosed the fateful lightning of His terrible swift sword.
> His truth is marching on.
> As He died to make men Holy, let us die to make men free!
> His truth is marching on
> Glory, glory! Hallelujah!
> Glory, glory! Hallelujah!
> Glory, glory! Hallelujah!
> His truth is marching on.

I felt the power of the Holy Spirit as the words filled the page. I felt calm and I was not afraid. I felt a peace I had not known for months. As I look back, I can see that this was a turning point. I could believe again that He would overcome my weakness and the desolation this disease had inflicted upon both my family and me. I could believe again that we would rise up out of the rubble and conquer this.

For with God, everything is possible. My faith will save me.

I feel your presence, Lord, like the power of a storm and want to know, love, and serve You. I stand in awe of your goodness and love and I know You will help me. I am here; I've come to do Your will.

The next day, I decided to call the Religious Education Office. I spoke with Thea and requested an Opening Prayer Special Announcement:

"Mrs. May is still hospitalized. If you wish to get in touch with her or if you have any questions, please continue to ask Mr. May or call Mrs. May and ask for the patient number."

The announcement was never made.

CHAPTER 23

MY THREE ANGELS

On October 5, 1989, the nurse told me Bill had called saying he would not be visiting for several days for a cooling-off period.

"That's okay, I know why Bill isn't visiting," I told the male nurse. The day before, Bill and I had argued over how long I would be in the hospital and what would happen after I left. And several days ago, I had been scolded about hugging and holding hands with a male patient. I had no recollection of doing this, but the nurses wouldn't make it up.

At 6:15 the next morning, while I was having my first cigarette of the day, I thought of Morse code. I had no idea as to why but decided to try to master this old method of communication. To this day, I still don't know if I wrote it correctly. I didn't know how to tap a key, but I wrote out dots and dashes, trying to write words into sentences. I spent the morning trying to perfect my new interest.

Late afternoon, Bill dropped the kids off at the unit, telling the nurse he would be back to pick them up, then left. "Mommy, give us a hug. We really miss you. When are you coming home?" I was delighted to see them.

Stephanie and Stacie did a lot of talking but Michael was generally quiet. I wondered what they were thinking, if they were still scared, if they could be honest with me about how they felt. I was feeling better, beginning to accept our family situation. Could we cope with the reality of my illness?

Bill returned about an hour later, stopped in, said little. I cried and cried as they left but was grateful that we would be together tomorrow even if for a brief time. I couldn't wait to go home.

I had been admitted on September 22, 1989, as an involuntary patient. On October 7, 1989, I was converted to voluntary status at this hospital for the mentally ill. I was given my rights and told that since it was a voluntary admission I could leave, but not for three days, as required by law. The doctor in charge then signed the notice.

The next time Bill and the kids visited, we needed to do something to put distance between ourselves and the situation. We composed a list of National Football League teams and who would be playing. I was taking my lithium daily and beginning to regain some of my competitive nature. We each made our own copy. I am not a football fan, but the idea of a contest of who could guess the most wins intrigued me. It gave us all something to do while we visited and showed everyone that Mom still had a sense of humor.

The day after, I had lunch with Bill off unit. We were both still on edge and only spoke briefly. When I returned, I kept a low profile and avoided staff contacts except for meeting physical needs. I was compliant with taking my medications. I was beginning to realize once again that I needed my lithium. I also attended a Mental Health Training group.

A nurse stopped me in the hall and asked me how the visit with my family went. "It was okay," I snapped, indignant at the constant intrusion into my affairs. I was feeling a sense of freedom, having been out. I resented hearing the door lock behind me. "We just have to work on a few things."

On October 10, I had lunch with Bill and kids in the hospital cafeteria. We ate in virtual silence. I felt very guilty. Bill toyed with his food and looked at the kids. I looked at Bill, wondering how we arrived here. *What did I do? What have I done to this family?*

They left immediately after lunch. I needed to do something to combat the sadness. I returned to my room and began writing in my journal.

"To Whom It May Concern: I would like to be discharged from Rochester General Hospital as soon as possible based on the evaluation of my physician/psychiatrist. Upon discharge, I would like to be enrolled in the Day Hospital Program T-TH."

The next morning, I had been up for an hour; the nurse had just left my room. One thing consumed my thoughts. *I have to behave myself to get out of this place. What do I have to do to go home as soon as possible?*

That same afternoon, a very dear friend, Jeanne, came to see me. She brought me some very colorful stationery and stickers of pink baby pigs. I remember smiling, shocked somewhere deep inside at feeling something akin to joy, being so appreciative that she would come and see me in this place. I often asked for Jeanne's help in religious and moral matters. I first met her in the late seventies, and over the years, I came to trust her judgment as fair and straightforward. Her visits brought with them a sense of sanity, that all was not lost, that I could carry on a conversation with friends, that I could return to normal.

One result of the conversation with my hospital psychiatrist earlier in the day was authorization for a community limit pass to go home from 5:20 p.m. to 7:30 p.m. Bill and Stacie came to pick me up. Walking through our front door, I felt anxious, like I was a visitor in my own home. The children stayed close to me, watching over their mother, and finished their homework in the dining room while we visited. I offered to help them. I wanted them to need me, but besides Stephanie who needed help with science, I could feel the distance created by this illness. I wanted to be involved in their daily lives; they didn't want to trouble their broken mother.

The time flew by and before I knew it, it was time for me to return to the hospital. We had moved into the living room. I sat on the sofa with Stacie, Stephanie, and Michael, making small talk like families do, when Bill came in and said that it was time to leave. I did not want them to see my disappointment, but tears rolled down my face. I held the three of them very close. They helped me up and we made our way to the front door.

"I'll be home way before Halloween. If there is a costume you can think of that I can make while I'm in the hospital . . ." Being home, even briefly, had revived some of my self-confidence. I had my arms around their shoulders as they walked in front of me toward the door. I was thinking of costumes for children; at the same time I felt as though they had to pretend to be adults for my sake. Their silence seemed to be confirming my fears. I wondered if they believed me.

I walked down the front steps. Bill was waiting in the car. I turned once more to look at Stephanie, Stacie, and Michael. "Please take care of Dad. I love you whole bunches and will be home very, very, soon. Mom will be home soon."

I heard the car door open and Bill's footsteps behind me. "We have to go back," he said as he took my arm and led me to the car.

"Bill, please don't make me go back, please don't make me go back."

On the way back to the hospital, I began to rant, telling him that he was to blame for me being in the hospital and that he shouldn't be taking me back.

He was driving about forty miles per hour on Cooper Road. "I'll jump!" I screamed. "I'm going to open the door and jump out of the car. I don't want to go back to the hospital. I want to stay home. I miss my kids. I don't miss you. But why should I?"

"Settle down, Joann." Grabbing my arm, he pulled me away from the door. "You will be home soon but you have to get better first." In hindsight I can see that he was trying to save me from myself. But at that moment, I hated him.

CHAPTER 24

A WRITTEN NOTE

The next morning, I was wide awake and restless by 4:45. I got up and walked to the nurses' station.

"Morning begins at 7:30," Nurse Diane said.

I went back to my room to look for something to do. I sat on my bed, turned on the radio, pulled a piece of paper from the nightstand, and started to write my name over and over: birth name, Americanized name, married name, Americanized married name, over and over. Who was I?

Lost in the music, I began to realize that I was feeling pretty good about myself. A few minutes later, another nurse came in to tell me to turn my radio down because they could hear it all the way down at the nurses' station. I was playing classic rock and actually felt alive again. I adjusted the volume and switched to a classical station. I was just as happy. I wrote in my journal:

My Dear Children,

It's very early and since I can't use the phone I'm writing to you. Keep praying and God will continue to bless us all. Your father and I love you all whole bunches.

I love you!
Mom

I also wrote a note to Bill. It expressed now lonely I felt without him and the children and asked him when the four of them would return. I missed them very much but realized that I needed to be hospitalized.

That afternoon, October 13, a tall gentleman walked into my room: "Hello Mrs. May, I am the staff attorney of the State of New York 4th Judicial Department. I am here to read you your rights as a mental patient." He conferred his official stamp of approval on my status. I had entered the hospital classified as involuntary until October 7, 1989. He helped me to realize that I was a patient, but a patient with rights. I could see some light, some hope. I was feeling better, but this was a confirmation that I was getting better, that others could see that I was getting better.

My psychiatrist stated that as there were no dangerous propensities, he would increase weekend pass limits to four hours on community leave with my husband.

The staff was looking after my care, observing my behavior, noting the progress and the dips. All I knew was that I felt a sense of liberty at now being voluntary, a sense of relief at the prospect of soon being able to go home, and at times a sense of frustration that I was not recovering faster. I sat down on my bed and wrote to my daughters and son.

The lithium was helping me get better and return to remission. I could still feel the swings in temperament, however, at times feeling as if I could control them, at others feeling as if they controlled me.

The following day, I was irritable, impatient, with rapid-fire monologue, while at other times I was cordial and friendly, appreciative of care.

Bill was trying to deal with home, the children, the hospital, doctors, and me. He was struggling too. At the time, I didn't care. I was mad at him.

On October 16, I left the dayroom. The psychiatrist had deemed me healthy. I was in remission. The lithium was working very well and I was given permission to sign out on community leave by myself.

I practically ran, bumping into people as I left the hospital. I felt freedom. I had no idea where I was going or what I was going to do. I just knew that freedom existed on the other side of those doors. I saw an RTS bus and, on impulse, decided to get on. I asked the driver where the bus was headed.

"Downtown Rochester."

I couldn't be happier. I had spent many a day shopping at Sibley's, McCurdy's, Foreman's, all of the clothing stores downtown. I slipped into a seat right behind the driver.

Fifteen minutes later, the bus stopped at Main and State. I was the first to get off. I walked through a warm October sun the short distance to Bill's workplace. I spotted a friend from the hospital using the phone outside the building. I waved to get his attention, but he waved me off, making it clear that he was busy. I was full of confidence coming into the city, but now I felt a little confused. In the midst of a crowd of strangers, I felt much less sure of myself and began to worry about which bus I would have to take to get back to RGH. I asked several people. Even if someone told me what I needed to know, I was confused.

It was then that I looked up at the white granite walls of Bill's office building and realized that my husband was working on the second floor. I immediately went up. He wasn't there. I never thought to ask anyone where he was. I sat and waited. I felt the anxiety rising in me. A part of me knew that my husband was not going to be very happy about this. Another part of me wanted to show him that I could take care of myself. A half hour later, Bill walked in. He drove me back to the hospital.

I don't know to this day what transpired between Bill and the staff on the unit. All I do know is that two days later I was cleared for discharge.

By the time of my discharge, dated October 18, 1989, I had been able to decipher and at times interpret my medical papers. Looking back, they helped to explain in greater detail what I suspected at the time. That initially I was experiencing a hypomanic attack, not a full-blown manic attack, and that I had bipolar. I did have panic attacks and felt very anxious. On a steady dose of lithium again, life gradually began to turn around. I now showed considerable progress with better organization and lucidity of thoughts. I was able to discuss disposition plans realistically and I showed concern for my family.

There were several meetings with Bill, the personnel, the doctors, and me, and one meeting with our family to discuss progress and problems leading to the hospitalization.

Upon discharge on October 18, I was encouraged to go to Day Hospital Entry Group meetings and I agreed to this, though I was not certain that I would have time or be able to tolerate this program after discharge.

Bill, Stephanie, Stacie, and Michael came to pick me up and take me home. I felt that I needed permission from the hospital to leave, but my husband reassured me that all the discharge papers had been signed and I would be home for good. The five of us ran like deer for our Plymouth Voyager. The ride home seemed to take forever. I grew more and more anxious. I glanced over my shoulder at the three happy children in the back seat. Still, I wondered: *What has this illness done to them?* I still do.

It was late that Wednesday afternoon by the time we got home. Some of the neighbors were out, but Kathy was the only one who came over. She and another neighbor, Sheila, had visited me in the hospital. I really appreciated their friendship.

We entered the house through the garage and went into the kitchen. The kids took me by the hand. "Mommy, we're so glad you're home, we really missed you."

"I missed you too." The tears of joy rolled down my cheeks.

Everyone cheered when Bill asked, "Who wants pizza?" Pizza is our favorite. Bill and Michael went to pick it up. The girls set the table and opened a two-liter bottle of soda, poured our drinks, and put them on the table. I was very tired and wandered around the kitchen trying to remember the last time we ate a meal at this table. We sat down as soon as they were home. First, we said grace and thanked God for all our blessings. While my family said grace, I couldn't stop thinking the following:

> *Lord, do You allow my pain in order for me to really appreciate my blessings? Without the pain I would not have such gratitude. My faith in You allows me to be conscious of Your plan for my life, and that plan includes the trauma and suffering of my bipolar illness. Denying this illness would be the epitome of hypocrisy on my part. I am your child and must accept myself for who I am. I have a hard time acknowledging my limits and that I have a need for healing, for medication, and for accepting your love. It takes great effort on my part to do this but with you, God, I will.*

Bill proposed a toast. "To Mom, the best mother in the whole world. She makes our family complete." Then we devoured our pizza.

The doorbell rang. I heard a voice down the hall as Bill opened the front door. My smoking buddy, Beth, rounded the corner and walked swiftly down the hall into the kitchen, smiling. Dressed casually in jeans and a T-shirt, she bubbled with enthusiasm, as she always did, warming me with her friendship, holding me together at times when I thought I would come apart. When she spoke, I listened, because I knew I could trust her. She had played a crucial role in having me go to the hospital.

"So glad to see you," she said. I stood up as she came to the table and gave me a hug. "Glad you're home. I missed you." She handed me a card.

The two of us walked out to the living room to chat, to catch up on lost time. She had not visited me while I was in the hospital, but it didn't make any difference. I always knew she was with me in spirit. I opened the card.

Dear Joann,

Just a card to say welcome home. We missed you and you were always in our prayers. Always remember that if you ever need anything, I will always be there for you.

Beth

Her sincerity showed through the words in the note and I knew that she meant them. She continued to visit me during the next few months and occasionally we would smoke a cigarette.

As months passed and I got better, we no longer smoked together in her basement, and once I got a teaching job, we didn't have the luxury of free time to spend together. We started to drift apart. Our family responsibilities and work undermined our friendship, but when I think of Beth, I think of the word *friend*. She helped me during a very difficult time of my life.

I awoke early on Thursday, the morning after I got home, and wanted to make homemade waffles with real maple syrup for breakfast. But Bill said, "You need to rest. The kids can make their own breakfast of cereal and toast." Which they did.

The children hugged me and said, "We're glad you're home."

"I love you all very, very much. You have to leave for school in a few minutes. Dad is driving you."

Bill went out first, started the car, and drove them to school instead of having them walk, so we could spend more time together. I kissed them as they ran out the door. I couldn't wait till the end of the school day. Bill came home after dropping them off.

Friday was a bright, warm, and sunny day for October. Stephanie, Stacie, and Michael wanted to walk to school with their friends. This was a good sign that perhaps they were okay. They had scrambled eggs and toast for breakfast, then brushed their teeth. I kissed them goodbye and then they were out the door.

Bill had made extra eggs and toast. After the kids left, we had the eggs with our second cup of coffee. We discussed my situation and our relationship. I was still very angry with him for making me go to the hospital. We talked about my CCD job and the fact that I was too sick to resume working at St. Thomas.

"You and the children are doing a great job, all of you enjoy it, and Father Callan approves of your work. It's more important that I stay home."

"Joann, I know you don't like to work outside, but how would you like to help me rake leaves today? The exercise alone would be good for you."

I agreed and we raked both the front and back yards. The colors of the leaves were radiant reds, yellows, and oranges just like a rainbow. They lifted my spirits. I looked up at the deep blue sky without a cloud in it and it renewed me. I once again thought of God and wondered where He would lead me. We finished raking right before Stephanie, Stacie, and Michael came running across the front lawn. They were excited to see me, and I was overjoyed to see them. Bill was in the garage and came out to greet them.

"How was everyone's day at school today?" I asked as I greeted each one on the front porch. They were hungry and thirsty and headed right to the kitchen.

The answers to my question would have to wait till they all got at least a drink first.

We sat around the kitchen table and I learned about their day. Bill stood behind me and put his hands on my shoulders. The children were happy, and their happiness made me happy. But in spite of this joyous occasion, my thinking still returned to my hospitalization. I couldn't get it out of my mind.

My memories of what happened while I was in the hospital and the events that happened in the months following my stay are more ambiguous than Bill's. My mood swings fluctuated between those that were despondent when I was in the gutter to those that were in the manic phase. I was very sad some days and very ecstatic on others. My actions demonstrated which mood swing I was in.

While I was still in the hospital, the lithium had kicked in, I was in remission, and I was "normal." After discharge I thought more of my family and less of me. In the weeks ahead, I enjoyed cooking, taking care of my family, and visiting with my family and friends. These visits were at times strained because even my close friends weren't quite sure of how to talk to me. And I wasn't sure about how much I wanted to share with them.

CHAPTER 25

BILL'S THOUGHTS
(OCTOBER 1989 – MARCH 1990)

It was good having Joann home. She loved being with the children and spent as much time with them as she could — and Stephanie, Stacie, and Michael loved being with their mother.

Although Joann was good with the children, there was definitely tension between her and myself. Joann still blamed me for her recent episode and said that I forced her to go to the hospital.

I had resigned from my job in September, around the same time that Joann had her manic attack. It was a blessing in a way so that I was home with the kids. I was getting them off to school, keeping up the house, and helping with the religious education program at St. Thomas.

The tension was getting worse between the two of us.

After Joann was discharged, she was scheduled to attend outpatient counseling at a Day Hospital Program that was set up by the hospital. I remember vividly her first and only appointment that she attended as an outpatient. It was scheduled for a week after she was discharged. The center was close to our house. Joann got all dressed up and was very quiet as I drove her to her appointment. It was a one-hour session. I dropped her off and said that I would be back in an hour to pick her up.

Upon my return, I walked into the center to wait for Joann's session to end. All of a sudden, Joann came charging out of the classroom yelling and cursing up a storm.

She said, "That was stupid and I'm not going back for any more sessions." She ran out to the parking lot heading toward a main road with heavy traffic. I ran after her, caught her, and held her tight to calm her down. She was extremely agitated and angry.

Finally I got her calmed down enough to get her in the car. I told her that I would be right back. I went back into the building to talk to her counselor. "Did you see what just happened? What do you plan to do to get her to come back for more therapy, which she definitely needs?"

The therapist just looked at me and said, "There is nothing else I can do if she does not want to come back for more help." The therapist was right, but I didn't see it that way. I was too angry.

"You must be kidding. This woman needs help and you are leaving it up to her if she wants therapy."

I walked out of the building in total disgust.

I went back to the car. Joann was still very angry and agitated. We drove around for a while until I felt that she was somewhat calmed down. She kept saying that she was never going back to that place nor did she want to see any other doctor. This really scared me. She would need a doctor to prescribe her meds, regulate her lithium levels, and provide her with necessary therapy. We had already seen what could happen if she did not take her lithium.

I was beside myself when we got home. I made some lunch and then Joann took a nap. She woke up when the kids came home from school and was somewhat relaxed. The kids did not know what happened that day, nor did they need to.

The next few days were very stressful between the two of us. If I felt that she was in a good place, I would bring up the subject of finding a new psychiatrist. This would get her angry as she swore she was not going to another doctor.

What could I do?

Joann and I still had Dr. John Ruef, our wonderful primary care doctor that we both respected. Maybe he could help. I mentioned this to her as a possibility that she would go and see him. She agreed to go. I called and made an appointment for the two of us. I mentioned to the receptionist the issue with Joann so that the doctor would have some indication of what was going on.

The next morning, Joann and I reached Dr. Ruef's office. She was relatively calm as we walked into his office building. I prayed to God that Joann would listen to Dr. Ruef and hopefully he could convince her to get help.

He came into the examining room, shook both our hands, and started to talk to Joann about what was going on in her life. She did not tell him everything.

He would look at me as if to say, "Is this everything?"

"No, Doctor." Then I proceeded to tell him the missing points. In his usual calming manner, Dr. Ruef spoke directly to Joann and asked her if she wanted to get better. She said that she did.

He recommended that Joann go and see Dr. Joseph Messina, a psychiatrist he was friends with who had helped some of his patients.

He gave us his address and phone number and suggested that we call him as soon as possible to set up an appointment. I think that Dr. Ruef was going to call Dr. Messina and tell him about Joann and to please accept her as a new patient.

I cannot thank Dr. Ruef enough for how he talked to Joann that day and got her thinking about getting better and that this could only be done with help. We shook hands and he wished us good luck as we left. Joann was calm for the first time in two months. She seemed to realize that yes, she did need help.

He continued to be our primary care physician until he retired. He was a kind, caring man.

When we got home, Joann called Dr. Messina's office to make an appointment. He could not see her right away because his schedule was full.

A letter dated November 20, 1989, confirmed her appointment with Dr. Messina. The appointment was for January 2, 1990, at 2:15 pm. He would be her psychiatrist now. Dr. Ruef gave her yet another referral.

When Joann had her initial appointment with Dr. Messina, I drove her to the appointment and waited in the lobby. When Joann came out, I asked her how it went. She said, "Okay." She scheduled her next appointment, which was a good sign. Joann continued to be under his care until he retired and moved out of state. February 27, 2008, was her last appointment with him.

She felt very comfortable with him. He monitored her lithium level and kept her in remission. With this help, Joann — and our relationship — also started to heal.

Dr. Messina was responsible for Joann getting her life back and her bipolar disorder under control. We knew that he would never try any experiments that would take Joann off lithium. For this we were all grateful. I am very appreciative for the compassion and time that Dr. Messina gave to Joann. I feel that he was the primary reason why Joann has been in remission all of these years.

I would not return to work full time until July of 1990. The time at home allowed me to help Joann and the kids and take care of what needed to be done there. Life was getting better every day. And by this time, Joann was healthy and normal enough to accept a teaching position herself.

CHAPTER 26

AT HOME WITH MY FAMILY

The second week of November 1989, Bill had another meeting with Father Callan, and it was again about me.

"Bill, I've been thinking about the future of our religious education program and am asking if your family can continue working till the end of the year. Let Joann stay home, rest, and take good care of herself. I am planning to hire another parishioner for Joann's position effective January first. You do understand, don't you?"

Bill was dumbfounded and at a loss for words, so he said nothing. He came home, and when we were alone, he told me the news.

Very hurt, I became despondent. During the months of November and December, I could hardly look at Father Callan and not want to ask, "Where is your compassion and understanding? Why did you fire me? Can't you see that I am getting back to normal? My family is doing an excellent job. I am fully capable of being coordinator."

I believed then, as I do now, that there is a reason for everything. We do not always know what the reason is, but, as I matured, my faith deepened and I relied more and more on the faith God gave me.

God, are you telling me to concentrate on my family? I do need to get over the hurt and think seriously about what needs to be done here at home. Help me, Lord, to live my life according to Your will. In order to do this, I need to take my lithium.

In the back of my mind I wondered, *Can I return to my teaching career?*

After the holidays, I updated my resume, and after discussing my plans with Bill and my children, I decided to start applying for a job.

We told Stephanie, Stacie, and Michael that effective

January 1, 1990, they would not be working at St. Thomas. This was a good opportunity to discuss my desire to return to teaching. In the process, Bill explained to them the status of my illness. He said to them, "As long as your mother is taking lithium, she is a normal and happy person. She has not been off of it since October of this past year and has not had any manic attacks during this time."

"We are proud of how well you are doing," they said.

"I am grateful for your understanding and love you very much," I said.

"We also think you should return to work."

"Thank you for your vote of confidence. I will start applying for a job during the next couple of months. I appreciate your support."

Perhaps Father did me a favor without intending to.

CHAPTER 27

TENURE

Dr. Messina ordered blood tests once a month starting in January 1990. I had to fast from lithium for twelve hours before my blood was drawn. He monitored the results, and by April, they showed that my level was stable. My behavior was back to normal and I was beginning to grow restless. On our way home from the lab one day, I expressed to Bill my desire to return to teaching. I had been thinking about it for several weeks, and besides, we needed the money. Bill agreed to discuss the possibility. We continued our discussion for several weeks weighing the pros and cons. We came to the same conclusion: I should apply for a teaching job for the following school year. I was still in love with teaching and my certification for Chemistry, Science 7–12, and Mathematics 7–12 was permanent. I was confident and eager to return to writing lesson plans, grading papers, and teaching a room full of students. Taking care of my family and my volunteer activities were very rewarding, but I wanted to do more with my life.

I decided to look for a teaching job in the educational system that I had taught in during the 1972–73 school year: the Roman Catholic Diocese of Rochester. I called the office to ask for an application. I completed it, answering all the questions, including the medical ones, and mailed it. I responded to the medical questions in such a way that my answers were truthful but did not reveal that I had bipolar. If I applied for a position today, I would answer honestly and not be afraid. I was anxious and spent the next few weeks waiting for the phone to ring.

Finally on a Monday, I got a call. "Hello, this is Sister Hughes from the Rochester Catholic Diocese general education office. Is this Joann May?"

"Yes."

Are you available to come in for an interview on Wednesday?"

"Yes, yes, I am."

"Then I'll see you at 9:30 a.m. sharp."

That morning, I started getting ready immediately after Stephanie, Stacie, and Michael left for school. Bill was home and offered to drive me. I said, "Thanks, but I want to drive myself." I fussed about what to wear and finally settled on a navy blue suit with a white blouse. This was very proper apparel for an interview, especially one for a Catholic school. I left at 8:30 and arrived for the interview with plenty of time to spare. The secretary said hello and offered me a seat. She was very friendly.

"Sister Hughes will be with you shortly."

"Thank you."

I was nervous until I met Sister. Ten minutes later, she invited me into her office. Standing about 5'6", she was a modern nun and was dressed in a gray suit and pink blouse. She wore a crucifix on a chain and a white veil over her light brown hair. She smiled and instantly put me at ease. She was younger than I had imagined, probably in her late thirties. During the interview I was relaxed and answered all her questions to the best of my ability.

"Joann, are you a practicing Catholic? Why do you want to teach and what is the greatest asset that you bring to the classroom?"

These were only a couple of the many questions Sister asked me that day. The interview ended on a positive note.

"You should hear from some of the principals who have openings."

We shook hands. I was confident that the interview was successful. I now had to wait for openings to occur in individual schools.

I waited and waited. About three weeks passed before I heard from any of the schools.

My first school interview was with the principal at St. Charles Borromeo Catholic School in Greece, New York. I learned later that she was a former nun. She was much shorter and older than Sister Hughes. She was also much more formal.

"What is your philosophy of education and why did you choose it as your career?"

"To be perfectly honest with you, I did not choose teaching as a career. I feel like it chose me. In 1970, I was a chemistry major in college and was planning a career in medical research. In August before my senior year, my advisor, Brother Simeon, asked me if I would be interested in teaching a high school chemistry class at Brunnerdale High School Seminary. I was working at a drugstore every weekend and anything sounded better than that. I interviewed with the principal, who was a priest . He was very charismatic and showed his enthusiasm for teaching. He also was very fond of his students. He offered me the position. I accepted and thus my teaching career was born."

Towards the end of the meeting, she asked, "Will you be able to teach Course One in math besides your science classes?"

In my mind I hesitated, but I said: "Yes, I am confident that I can."

"My main difficulty has been to find a math teacher. You are the first candidate who is certified for both science and math."

"Yes, I am."

"Then you are hired. Welcome to our team."

In September 1990, I began teaching sixth-, seventh-, and eighth grade-science; Course One in math; and a reading class for the 1990–91 school year. I had a good year and spearheaded the school's very first science fair for grades kindergarten through eight. I worked with my students and the other teachers worked with theirs under my guidance. My students became teachers for a day and explained their projects to fellow students, family, and friends. For example, two seventh-grade girls did their project on blood pressure. They learned how to take it, brought a cuff to the fair, and practiced on family and friends. They were so proud, and so was I. Everyone received many accolades that evening. My family attended and cheered me on. This was the life I wanted to live.

CHAPTER 28

STACIE'S PHONE CALL

My life was full, perhaps too full, and at the end of the school year I re-evaluated my position. I loved my job, but the pressure and stress of preparing five different lessons and grading all those papers was beginning to take a toll on me.

In the summer of 1991, I resigned my position at St. Charles and applied at Northeastern Catholic Junior High, also a diocesan school, for the following school year. It wasn't that I didn't like it at St. Charles, but at Northeastern I would get a decrease in the number of subjects that I would be required to teach. I would only be teaching seventh-grade life science and eighth-grade physical science. The only trade-off was the number of students. I would have a total of a hundred and fifty students instead of seventy-five. I taught at Northeastern from September 1991 through June 1995.

By that time, two of our children were in college. I needed to be more pragmatic. I spent the summer of 1995 completing applications for public school positions and going on every interview I was granted. I was confident that I would get a position, but by the end of August, I still didn't have a job and it was time to take Stacie to the University of Scranton in Pennsylvania for her freshman year.

On August 19, Bill and I drove Stacie to college. She arrived a week early to participate in the cross-country team's annual training camp in Canada. After Stacie met her roommates and organized her room, we had a bite to eat, kissed her goodbye, and began our four-hour journey home. We arrived home around 5:00 p.m. We relaxed and began to prepare dinner.

Around 7:00 p.m. that night, we received a phone call. It was from Stacie. Her first words were: "I'M OKAY. We were underwater, but now I'm okay."

She went on to tell us how she was riding in a van with nine other female runners when the driver plunged the van off the road and into fifteen feet of water in Wolf Lake near Westport, Ontario. She said, "As the van sank, I struggled to unbuckle my seatbelt. I was drowning and thought I would die. Steve, our coach, who was riding in a van in front of ours, noticed that we were not behind him. He turned around just in time to see the van go under. It was very quick action on his part that saved us. He took a large rock, threw it in, and broke the windshield. This allowed me and eight other runners to float to the top, catch our breath, and swim to safety." Two of the girls were unconscious and had to be pulled out of the van. They remained in the hospital for an extended stay but were later okay.

"We were all soaking wet and our bags were at the bottom of the lake. After examining us, the doctor told us we were fine. The hospital gave us each two gowns to wear. We were quite a sight, standing on the sidewalk outside the hospital."

Bill and I were shocked and our knees were shaking. "Are you sure you're all right? When can we come and get you?"

"They want us to stay here for a couple of days and then we can come home."

We got down on our knees and thanked God for sparing our daughter.

After picking up Stacie, Bill, the kids, and I stayed home together for several days.

We expressed our deepest gratitude for saving our daughter's life to Steve, her coach, in a letter written on August 30, 1995:

Dear Steve,

We've had some time to pray and reflect on the August 19 accident and know in our hearts that if it wasn't for you and Mike, the girls would not be alive today. No amount of time can completely erase the fear of what could have happened but DIDN'T. When Stacie called, we thought she was making a routine phone call. But she explained further and gave us some of the details. The words resounded then and still do now: "MOM. I'M OKAY. I'M OKAY. WE WERE UNDERWATER BUT NOW I'M OKAY. I DIDN'T EVEN NEED STITCHES."

Our first reaction was to come and get her and bring her home. It was difficult to stay put and respect her wishes to stay at the camp. We know now that it was the right thing to do.

No one knows or understands the mind of God, but He allowed the accident to happen and then allowed everyone to live for a definite reason. Stacie will look at her life and the world differently. We are once more reminded that all life, including our own, is a gift from God.

I applied to Wheatland–Chili Central School District while Stacie was home, after reading their ad for a junior high science teacher position in the *Democrat and Chronicle*. I completed an application and sent my resume along with a cover letter. I was granted two interviews during the third week of August: the first one with the superintendent, the second with the principal and the teacher-hiring committee. They must have been satisfied with my answers to their many questions because I was offered the position. I signed my contract in late August and couldn't believe that my pay almost doubled and my student load decreased from a hundred and fifty students to seventy-six students.

I began a successful eleven-year teaching career at Wheatland–Chili Junior-Senior High School in Scottsville, New York, teaching seventh-grade life science and eighth-grade physical science. They were the same courses I had previously taught in my other schools. Occasionally, I was asked to teach chemistry.

One of my chief accomplishments was to put on a successful science fair for the first four or five years. The students worked on their projects from October to May and were very proud of their work. By the time they finished, they knew the scientific method inside and out.

Science teachers from other schools served as judges and we awarded prizes for first, second, and third place and several honorable mentions. The school day ended at 2:05 p.m. and judging took place from 4:00 to 6:00 p.m. The students went home at the end of the day and returned dressed in their Sunday best for the judging. The science fair was open to the public all evening. It was quite an elaborate affair with high school students displaying projects too.

Besides the science fairs, my eighth-grade students also made solar cars as part of their physical science curriculum. The school provided the panels and the students used their own materials to make the cars. We raced them on a bright sunny day in the spring with the seventh graders cheering their favorite cars on. The other Wheatland–Chili science teachers were the judges. Select students also entered their solar cars at the Rochester Institute of Technology (RIT) E[3] Fair, an event showcasing student engineering projects as well as demonstrations from professional engineers.

On June 1, 1999, after completing my third year of teaching in Wheatland, I received a letter from my superintendent:

The Board of Education of the Wheatland–Chili Central School District on May 25, 1999, accepted the recommendation of the superintendent of schools to approve your tenure appointment effective September 1, 1999. In taking this action, the Board of Education acknowledged your effectiveness and contributions as a teacher in the science area. Congratulations on reaching this important milestone in your educational career at Wheatland–Chili.

Your tenure appointment becomes effective upon your return to a teaching position in September 1999 and with the submission of the attached medical form. The district will reimburse the cost of the medical exam not covered by insurance. Again, congratulations and best wishes for the remainder of the year.

After a brief moment of elation, fear flooded my entire body. They wanted this medical form completed by my doctor. The question I feared the most was: "Have you ever been treated for a mental illness?" I could only answer it with a yes or no. Throughout my teaching career, I never revealed the fact that I suffered from bipolar disorder. But now there was no other way of getting around the cold, hard truth. I had to submit this medical report from my doctor before the district could complete my tenure process.

When I brought the form to Dr. Messina, I asked, "What do I do?"

"Tell the truth."

"I don't want to, but I have to, don't I?"

After much discussion he completed the form, and the next day I gave it to our superintendent. Inside, I was shaking like a leaf. On the outside, I was calm and confident.

"How many other people are privy to this information?" I asked.

At that time, I was not cognizant of the Americans with Disabilities Act of 1990, which took effect July 26, 1992. It prohibits private employers, state and local governments, employment agencies, and labor unions from discriminating against qualified individuals with disabilities in job application procedures, hiring, firing, advancement, compensation, job training, and other terms, conditions, and privileges of employment.

My disability didn't interfere with my work. I confess that a couple of times a semester, I took a day off to regroup when I was teaching. This action contributed to my success. I loved my students but they did take a lot of my energy.

I did not lose my job and I did receive tenure. But still, every day I wondered, was it because of this federal law that I received tenure, or would I have received it anyway without it?

I continued to teach seventh-grade science for seven years. They were good years and I continued to sponsor science fairs except for the last couple of years, due in part to the increased testing on the state level that left a lack of necessary time for projects. I taught until July 1, 2006, when I officially retired after eleven years in the Wheatland–Chili Central School District.

During these years I also thought that I would like to be an administrator, so I started taking graduate courses in administration at the University of Rochester. I earned my certificate in 2006. The same year I retired from teaching I started looking for a principal's or vice principal's position.

I would like to say that everything went well, but I can't. I became despondent and unsure of myself. I had several interviews and I failed all of them. I simply could not project myself as knowledgeable, decisive, and sure of myself. By September of 2006, I decided to stop looking for an administrative job. Instead I decided to substitute at local middle and high schools. I did that for about five years.

CHAPTER 29

REMISSION

I have been in remission while taking lithium since 1981, except for a short time in 1989. While in remission, I have cared for my family and volunteered in the church, school, and community. I pursued my teaching career for many years and was very happy doing so. My family has grown. My three children are all successful and I have six grandchildren. My children have survived my illness and show me a lot of understanding. They have a lot of empathy toward others and Bill and I are very proud of them. They treat me with respect and give me hugs when I'm with them.

It is only because of lithium that I have been successful, especially in the classroom, and continue to have a happy and healthy life. I now accept myself, and although I don't shout at the top of my lungs that I have bipolar disorder, if someone asks, I tell them.

But lithium isn't a miracle drug without any repercussions. If someone takes too much, they can get lithium poisoning.

I was told about lithium poisoning but never thought it could happen to me. But it did: I had lithium poisoning in January 2014. My internist had me tested for Parkinson's because I had all the symptoms: I dropped my coffee cup, nothing would stay in my hands, I couldn't walk in a straight line. This scared my husband and me to death.

What follows is Bill's recollection of the episode.

CHAPTER 30

BILL'S DESCRIPTION OF MY LITHIUM POISONING

It was sometime during September 2014 that I started to notice that Giovanna was acting differently. She blinked her eyelids constantly and was scuffing her shoes. She also showed signs of forgetfulness and was questioning herself about what she was doing almost daily. This was not like her at all. She had always showed confidence and independence in her daily routines. I noticed that Giovanna was dropping items regularly and her behavior was changing.

Our entire family was going to be home for Thanksgiving. This holiday had in the past been a wonderful and happy time for Giovanna. She loved making up the menus for the week and would ask for input from our children. Giovanna started planning the menu in October. A usually somewhat easy task became a torture for her. She was changing the menu almost weekly and worried that it was not going to satisfy everyone. It got to the point that it was annoying both for myself and Stacie. We kept assuring her that whatever she made for the week would be wonderful. Giovanna doubted herself. In addition, her other symptoms I had noticed earlier were getting worse. Both Stacie and I attributed these issues to the fact that everyone was going to be home: eight adults, five grandchildren, and a dog. Well, Thanksgiving was a huge success, as always, and afterwards she seemed to calm down a bit and was more relaxed. Giovanna didn't seem to think that anything was wrong.

Christmas Day went well without much of an issue for Giovanna. We had dinner on Christmas Eve with Stacie and her husband, Mike. The four of us shared a relaxing evening together. Christmas Day started out with our attending Mass at St. Thomas the Apostle with Stacie. We had a light brunch after Mass and later in the day visited our dear friends Bob and Kathy for a delicious Christmas dinner.

New Year's Day was wonderful—a quiet dinner, just the two of us. But Giovanna was still showing signs of scuffing her feet, still showing extensive blinking and signs of forgetfulness.

I was concerned with these symptoms and kept praying that they would go away soon. Giovanna wanted to visit her mother and sister in Ohio for New Year's. Unfortunately the weather was not cooperative.

We waited to see what the weather was going to be like. Giovanna was in no way capable of driving herself. I told her that I would go with her for the weekend. The weather cooperated and we left on Friday morning, January 16, 2015. Giovanna was not herself. She was more nervous than usual.

On Sunday, Giovanna wanted to make a birthday cake for her sister. Lucy was going to be out for three to four hours, so she thought it would be a perfect time to make the cake and surprise Lucy when she came home. Giovanna would normally whip up a cake in minutes, but it wound up being a difficult task for her. Of course, not knowing where the bowls, mixer, and utensils were at her sister's house did not help the matter. The final result was far from her best. I felt so bad for her. She was struggling and she knew it.

Giovanna was in constant stress. I cannot believe that neither her sister nor her mother noticed anything about how she was feeling or how she was behaving. It was obvious that she was not herself. I could not wait to leave and get Giovanna home.

We stayed until Monday. When we got home, I couldn't help noticing that things were getting worse. Giovanna could not face her symptoms, psychological or physical. One noticeable change was her tendency to drop items she held. I was at work one day in January when I received a call from her. She was panicking.

"Slow down. What's up?" I asked.

She said that she dropped her full coffee mug. Coffee had spilled all over the end table in the living room. Giovanna clearly had no idea what had just happened to her. She was afraid and called her doctor to make an appointment. This was the first time she acknowledged something was wrong. I was very grateful that she came to this conclusion and made the appointment to see her primary doctor as soon as possible.

The day of her appointment, I was a nervous wreck. I offered to go with her but she wanted to go alone. I knew something was medically wrong but had no idea how serious it could be. Every time my phone rang at work, my heart jumped. Finally, I received her call.

She spoke, but I heard only one word: *Parkinson's*. I was speechless.

Her doctor scheduled an MRI and wanted Giovanna to see a neurologist. I felt that was a good start. When I got home, I tried to ask her questions about what the doctor said. She did not want to discuss the matter. I think that I let it go. Later that night I went on to the computer to research Parkinson's disease. It was frightening. The symptoms were apparent in Giovanna's current state. Later she came over to sit next to me. Together we spent the balance of the evening reading about this disease.

I took Giovanna to get her MRI a week after her appointment with her primary care physician, and within a couple of days, we received the good news that it was *not* a tumor, which was a relief.

Our next step was to meet with the neurologist, Dr. Evans. Giovanna asked if I would go with her to her appointment. He was very cordial to both of us. He referred to her primary doctor's notes as well as her recent MRI results. He asked Giovanna how she was feeling, what changes she had been experiencing recently. He ran other tests in his office: muscle coordination and eye function, her manner of walking and sitting. He reviewed her current list of medications and started out by mentioning Parkinson's disease as a possibility. However, he emphasized that this disease is often misdiagnosed due to current medications taken by a patient who has bipolar. Some medications, if overdosed, can definitely mimic symptoms of Parkinson's. He specifically zeroed in on two medications: lithium and olanzapine. He suggested that Giovanna make an appointment with her psychiatrist as soon as possible for blood work to determine her levels of lithium and olanzapine. An overdose of either of these medications can cause Parkinson's-like symptoms. He would forward with his observations. We felt a bit uplifted. Dr. Evans was encouraging and appeared very thorough in his diagnosis.

After leaving Dr. Evan's office, Giovanna called her psychiatrist to set up an appointment at the earliest opportunity. Little did I know that she took it upon herself to play doctor and stopped taking the olanzapine. Giovanna needed this medication to help her deal smoothly with life's highs and lows. She had a blood workup prior to her appointment. I did notice that she was not herself. Now Giovanna could not sleep and said she felt that her brain was coming apart. When her psychiatrist saw the blood results, she called and told her to stop taking the lithium altogether for twenty-four hours and then take only 450 mg per day and start taking the olanzapine again. Her psychiatrist made it perfectly clear in no uncertain terms that she should never have stopped taking the olanzapine.

The psychiatrist was calming but definitely concerned about Giovanna's current mental state. The lithium level was close to being dangerous. Another couple of days without proper care and Giovanna would have been in the hospital for lithium poisoning. Her doctor was having additional blood work drawn over the next month to monitor her lithium levels.

We left the doctor's office somewhat relieved. Giovanna was to start taking her olanzapine immediately. We were told that Giovanna should notice a difference in clarity within hours. The higher level of lithium would take a few days to level off to the proper level.

We relaxed when we got home. Maybe the neurologist was correct in his diagnosis that her issues over the past several months were from her medications.

Within a couple of days there was a noticeable change for the better in Giovanna's overall mental and physical daily routines and clarity in her speech and thinking. She was no longer scuffing her feet, and her excess blinking had decreased a great deal. Things were somewhat getting back to normal at home. I could breathe a bit easier and did not panic every time my phone rang at work. I must say that Giovanna's psychiatrist stayed on top of this matter and kept her primary care physician and neurologist updated throughout this process.

We had a follow-up appointment with the neurologist somewhere around four to six weeks after her initial visit. By then Giovanna was showing definite signs of improvement. He ran the same tests and at the end he felt confident that she did not have Parkinson's but rather lithium poisoning. We could not thank him enough for his diagnosis that led to Giovanna's recovery. He is a very caring and thoughtful physician.

Our son, Michael, who lives in Virginia, was concerned about his mother. He wanted to come home for a visit during his mother's illness but unfortunately was not able to. He talked his mother into going down for a week in early September to spend time with his family. She originally hesitated, but we convinced her that she was getting stronger and the visit with her grandchildren would do her good. It wound up being a great prescription for her. She came home much better mentally, physically, and spiritually.

In conclusion, this episode in Giovanna's life was very serious and sudden. The end result wound up being fine but what it could have been is a frightening thought.

Bill's account of what happened to me due to the lithium poisoning helped me to realize that I really do suffer from bipolar disorder and need to monitor my lithium. While I suffered from lithium poisoning, I wasn't thinking clearly and had a car accident. I was a danger behind the wheel. Thank God no one got hurt. I have suffered for many years with bipolar disorder but never had lithium poisoning before this incident, which turned out to be a very frightful experience. Now I know the signs to look out for to avoid it getting bad in the future.

CHAPTER 31

A TRIP TO MY MOTHER'S

Although it was a rainy fall afternoon, I decided not to use an umbrella as I got out of my car. The six-hour trip had been routine for years as a family. Now that the children had grown and moved on, I was making it alone about once a month.

When my mother called, she said she had something important to talk about. As I knocked on her front door, my hands began to tremble. I didn't know what mood she would be in. She was ninety years old. Her purpose had always revolved around her family, her faith, and a tenacious opinion as to how the world should turn.

I heard her hand on the brass knob and the varnished door slipped open. She offered me a hug. I smiled and hugged her back.

"Come in, come in," she said with lukewarm enthusiasm. Still the lover of fashion, she was dressed in gray slacks and a gray and white flowered cardigan over a white satin blouse. She stood aside as I entered.

My mother followed me into the kitchen. The overhead light reflected her shining curly white hair. She was aging like an olive tree, bending to the years, the hardships, the passing of generations, but within her, the vigor and determination of her prime remained. I sat down at the kitchen table. She stood opposite me, leaning into the table on her hands. Her almond skin was thinning and creased but still soft.

"You've been drinking coffee since you were four years old," she said, with a trace of a smile through the sadness of her eyes—a trace of the joy those eyes once wore in the fields of Italy. "With lots of milk and sugar. I bought some Italian cookies yesterday. Okay?"

"Sure, Mom."

"I'll pour us some coffee." She hobbled over to the counter. "The almond ones are really delicious."

Growing up, I often felt stifled from her overprotection. But over the years, she had withdrawn more and more into herself. Mother still related to the world, but more and more so through the lens of a life already lived.

She still sewed and crocheted and cooked to keep herself busy, but when we talked, she was fond of remembering her years in Italy. At times, she would get up and look out the window, get a glass of water, or check the laundry. But she would always return to her chair to remember.

"We were young and foolish." When she spoke of the memories deepest in her, her eyes would focus on the emptiness of the air around us as she drew those tales to the surface of her life once again. "During the war, we would work in the fields of our farm and watch the bombs go off in the distance. We danced around in the fields, sang songs, and laughed. My sisters and I had no idea of the danger we were in."

The memories began to slip by like the billboards so long ago on the train from Aielli to Naples — her vigor in the fields of Italy, our voyage to America, her talent as a dress designer and seamstress, the catalogue of dresses she made for my sister and me throughout the years.

I sewed my first dress for a 4-H fashion show with her help. In the early 1960s, I strutted through Sundays in a pink suit and matching pillbox hat identical to Jackie Kennedy's. My prom dress and my wedding gown were all Mom's work.

She got up then slowly tottered her way back with a couple of hatboxes. "I knew I had them. I just couldn't remember where. I'm too short to see the shelf in my closet. Your brother-in-law found them for me." She slid the coffee cups to one side and set the boxes down.

Mother sat down and pulled out three-inch bundles of envelopes tied with white ribbon. "Letters from your father after he left for America . . ." She set them to one side, slid a box in front of me, nibbled cookies and sipped coffee.

I started removing the black-and-white photos from the boxes, sorting through a few at a time. I had seen them before: photos of my mother's family in Italy both before and after we left, photos of relatives I didn't know — whom my mother would try and relate to me, photos that brought the past back to life. A professional photo from Rome of my cousins Erminia and Elisa in dress clothes. I had wanted to be like them because they each had a doll. My favorites have never changed — Papa Domenico when he attended a VFW reunion, and Zio Luigi, my dad's brother, with Lucia and me. He was father to us during my dad's two years in America before we joined him. He was the man I looked up to and saw every day in my father's place.

Mom rose and drifted to the counter to stir sauce on the stove and putter with chores. I thumbed through the box. My father's passport appeared among the cluster of photos. I opened it, looked at the photo — he was twenty-nine and a very handsome man — and handed it to my mother.

"Your father was a very sick man." She looked at the table in the same way she would if she were studying the layout of a dress pattern, with more resignation in her voice than fondness. "It's what made him drink too much and behave the way he did. But he was also a very good man who helped others. He always attended eight o'clock Mass at St. Francis Xavier Church on Sundays. He always sat in the last pew."

Mother handed me the passport. "Here, I don't need this anymore. It's not going to bring him back." She set the photographs down and picked up her coffee cup as if for just a moment, the pictures were too near the memories.

This is the story she always told. Mussolini's army took Papa to Bari, Italy, and trained him to be a telegraph operator. He served in Greece. When the Allies invaded in the south of Italy, Mussolini went north and kept the north of Italy tied to Hitler. The Germans gave Italian soldiers a choice: fight for Germany, or be imprisoned or killed.

They moved through prison camps. My father saw what Hitler was doing, killing people by the trainload, forcing people to dig their own graves for their own executions. He worked as slave labor in the coal mines and watched boxcars loaded with dead bodies arrive to be incinerated in the camp's ovens.

She returned to the photos, flipping to one of the *Andrea Doria*, the ship that brought us to America.

"Your father, you, and your sister before he left . . . our passport photo . . ."

"Look how stern we look, Mom." We did, as if to relax and smile for an official photo were a violation of an Italian eleventh commandment.

"You, Lucy, and I went to Naples by train about six months before to get physicals for our trip to America. Your Papa Domenico came with us and watched over us. The gypsies in Naples were famous for stealing wallets. When we returned to Aielli, you ran into the Campomizzi house and shouted to Papa Giovanni and Mamma Victoria, 'I am going to see Papa and I'm going to America!' Mamma Victoria patted you on the head and said, 'Rodolfa will never leave Italy.' They were always against me."

I picked out a photo of my mother with her coworkers at an employee luncheon for Stern and Mann's, the Canton department store where she had worked many years later. Seated at a restaurant with two other women who smiled into the camera, my mother's face and eyes were as vacant as a mannequin's.

"This is from when I had my head injury and I was sick the first time, isn't it?" I handed her the photo.

"Yes, it was a tough time. We didn't know what was happening. I didn't want anyone to know that we didn't know."

Time froze. The present disappeared. Even now, forty-five years later, the memory of the hospitalization was as real as when it happened. "I still can't believe that you and Dad allowed it. The treatments were so painful. All that electricity surging through you. It's like being executed, but you don't die."

Mom turned and looked at me, then back at the photo. "I visited you every day," she said, but we both knew it wasn't true, and she wasn't able to look me in the eyes.

"You never mentioned how the treatments affected you. How could I know? Dr. Beshara said that without them you wouldn't be normal for the rest of your life. I was so scared. Your dad and Lucy were scared. I don't even think Lucy really knew what was going on." Her words were slow and deliberate. "We just wanted you to be better."

"What do you mean you didn't know?" That first hospitalization began a lifetime of simmering anger over the pain of it all. My anger was a lingering reminder of the guilt I felt, that I had somehow brought this on myself, and here it was again. "Didn't you have to know before they could treat me?"

"When you get sick, you think maybe you'll get over it. When your children get sick, you do what the doctor tells you."

"What good did it do?"

"What do you mean?" she asked. "You had the best doctor, the treatments worked, you're normal now." She got up and stirred the sauce. "Why are you talking like that? There's nothing wrong with you. My doctor told me years ago that you were okay if you took your medicine."

"I know you had a good reason. I know you love me. But your doctor isn't a psychiatrist. I've lived with this my entire adult life. Do you think I might have some idea of how it feels, that what I have is managed, not cured? You saw the outside of me. If I looked healthy, you thought that I was getting better. But you never saw the inside, the impact those treatments had on me, still have on me."

I could feel the desperation rising, the current of self-inflicted shame on which the course of my life rode for decades. But there was no use trying to explain any of this to my mother. I had felt alone for what seemed like forever: three weeks in the hospital and four months at home. Mom and Dad worked. My sister was in school. I had hours each day trying to put the pieces of my life back together. The silence of others and solitude within taught me I should be ashamed of what I'd become.

Mother crossed from the stove to the table with a tablespoon of sauce. "Taste . . . does it need anything?"

"You never told anyone. You treated me like this was something physical, something I would get over. But you treated it 'out there,' like it was something different, something to not talk about, something to be ashamed of."

"We had to work. We didn't realize that you were lonely."

She walked over to the front window. A light rain still fell. The leaves in the trees were just beginning to turn. "Giovanna, we felt helpless, that we had no choice. Your father and I thought that you needed time to rest, to recover, and then you would get better. You had a future. This is a small town. We told who we had to."

"Like who?"

"Our health insurance wouldn't cover electric shock treatments. We went to Mr. Hoffee, the president of the bank, and told him that you had a serious fall at college. We needed a loan to pay for the treatments to make you better. Without any hesitation he said, 'Of course you can borrow the money.'"

"You never told me about a loan."

"There are a lot of things I never told you, Joann."

My mother was right. There were many times throughout our lives when silence was her defense, when the only way to try to understand her was to read her expressions, watch how she moved, and wonder what was happening behind the look in her eyes.

She stepped back over to the table, noticing our passport from 1954 among the photos.

"Here, take this," she said.

"Are you sure you want me to take this? Don't you want to keep it?"

I wanted the passport. It meant a lot to me. It reminded me of Italy, of being an American, of everything America stood for. It represented a lot of memories: our new dresses made by my aunt for our adventure to America, my education. Mrs. Looby, our first-grade teacher who used to play the violin for us in class. I had never heard a violin before. My education right through college—so many events in my life that never would have come to be in a small town in the mountains of Italy. I wanted to remember that the passport in my hands had been an opportunity not everyone was given. And that there had been a time before I was broken in two.

My mother, Rodolfa Palerma Campomizzi, grabbed the booklet of Erminia's pictures and added them to her pile of photos we were returning to the boxes. Then, becoming a little anxious, she walked over to one of the kitchen drawers and took out some pills. Noticing a couple of breadcrumbs on the floor, she bent over to pick them up. "You keep it. The dreams were much prettier than the reality."

CHAPTER 32

THE PRESENT

In September 2006, I joined the Osher Lifelong Learning Institute at the Rochester Institute of Technology and started writing my memoir. I needed to write about my bipolar disorder and share my story in order to get rid of the self-inflicted stigma I felt. This was very difficult to do, but gradually by the end of the semester I succeeded.

As I wrote, thought, and shared, my guilt and shame started to dissipate. By writing this book, it finally sank in that what I had was a biological disease caused by a chemical imbalance in the brain, not a personality defect. Gradually accepting this has given me peace and a healthy attitude. This peace has stayed with me for many years.

I now sit here in a coffee shop in Upstate New York, finishing this story, remembering a trip across the ocean to my new home, how the keepers of destiny wove the strands that led me here, how so many have tried and continue to try to find a place in this land of tortured dreams, but dreams nonetheless. I wonder if my own children have fulfilled their dreams and if they are happy. They say they are and that I touched their lives in a good and positive way. I like to think that this is true. But as I sit here, where I have had coffee with Stacie on many occasions, I ponder how my keepers of destiny were also those for Stephanie, Stacie, and Michael.

We all wanted to believe, to hope, that the events of the past would be left there. The children talked to and comforted each other. The three of them did very well in school, played with their friends, participated in sports, and performed their assigned chores at home. Looking back, I wish I had spoken with them more about my illness when they were children instead of waiting until they became adults.

Several years ago, my then-forty-year-old daughter Stephanie was visiting from Minnesota for Thanksgiving.

"Do you remember when I used to go to Mrs. Bain's after school?" she asked from the dining room.

I was cleaning up in the kitchen. We were the only two in the house. I heard the quiver in her voice. She hesitated, as if she was not sure she should ask. I knew right away that she was referring to my hospitalization at Strong Memorial Hospital in 1981.

"Yes, I remember." I walked into the dining room. She was standing, leaning on one of the chairs, and looking at the piano. She turned toward me, her voice softer than normal.

"Mom, how old was I when you were sick?"

"Stephanie, you were seven years old. It was my 1981 attack."

"Is that why I had to go to Mrs. Bain's after school?"

A sense of relief flooded over me. "Yes, that's why you had to go to Mrs. Bain's."

"I remember Mrs. Bain."

"She was a wonderful neighbor. She helped Dad while I was in the hospital." I saw the pain in my daughter's heart. I walked closer and pulled her to me. "You must have been so scared and confused" We both fought back tears. I let go of her to look into her eyes, then hugged her again. "I'm so sorry for all the pain I caused you."

I felt a stab of guilt. Oh my God, I was angry with my mother for not telling anyone about my head injury and subsequent hospitalization. I realized that I had been doing the same thing with my own family by remaining silent.

I had tried so hard to keep my condition secret, knowing that I was denying what my family already knew. I was so relieved that the truth was out in the open. A weight lifted from me now that the truth was out.

"I know my behavior has been difficult on the three of you and Dad. At times, my life was a living hell and at others it was marvelous."

Stephanie gave me a pat on the back and smiled with her eyes, a smile that said, *I understand.* I looked out the window.

I couldn't look her in the eyes; I knew I would break down. I wanted it to all be over. I wanted the pain to go away. I wanted to be relieved of the guilt I felt. I wanted to love my family without the burden of what I had put them through.

My daughter was taking this on with me. She chose to allow me to be honest and in so doing was willing to share the pain.

I looked back at her and saw the tears. I whispered, "You suffered all these years . . . you didn't understand the reason for that suffering."

"You had to live through the pain that it caused."

I felt the silence between us.

"Stephanie, no matter what, I love you and never meant to hurt you. I have a mental illness."

We were both crying.

"Mom, I love you."

I loved her the moment I knew she existed. I loved her when I first laid eyes on her, a beautiful baby with pure pink skin and beautiful black hair. Her first cry was music to my ears. She made me a mother. She grew and became wise. I loved her then, and even more now.

"You remember how difficult 1989 was. Your father thought I was having a manic attack, but I didn't lose touch with reality, so I thought it couldn't be. As I look back, I should have known something wasn't right."

"We could see it too, Mom. We just didn't know what to do."

"Stephanie, I didn't wish my bipolar disorder upon myself, but I wish I had been more open with you, Stacie, and Michael from the beginning. From now on I will be honest with the three of you. Ask me any question and I will do my best to answer it."

"Thanks, Mom." She smiled.

Many years have passed and I have a lot to be thankful for. I have been in remission from bipolar disorder for about thirty years. My lithium level has to be monitored every month or two to make sure it doesn't rise to the poisoning level. Since my lithium poisoning in 2014, I had another relapse of poisoning in 2019. Kate Schroeder-Bruce, my nurse practitioner, acted very quickly and had me go off the lithium until my level got back down, then lowered the dosage. I am feeling fine now.

My husband and I are both retired and are enjoying our children and grandchildren. Stephanie, Stacie, and Michael have matured into wonderful adults in spite of the challenges they faced due to my illness.

EPILOGUE

I have prayed and prayed for many years, almost on a daily basis. I have asked God to take away the pain and the stigma of my mental illness, or the illness itself. So far He has not. I turn my prayers around and ask that if He won't take away my illness and my pain, would He at least help me to cope with this torture?

I find that the pain is worse when I am depressed. I am sometimes so depressed that I cannot get out of bed, take a shower, or perform any daily chores. I try to give myself some worth by repeating to myself: "I am a child of God, I am a Child of God, I am a child of God." I scream and I gnash my teeth. "Please make the pain go away." The pain does subside and I experience periods of time that are somewhat normal. During these rather tranquil times, I was able to take care of my husband and three children and even work. I was able to teach. I was able to live a life.

If I have been given life in order to learn, I have carried along a soul on the wind of a love that I cannot explain. I have learned to dream and to believe the dream beyond the sorrows of life. This illness has helped me increase my faith and appreciation for God, my life, family, and friends.

I accept my life as it is and has been.

A MEDITATION
by Cardinal John Newman

GOD has created me to do Him some
definite service; He has commanded some
work to me which He has not committed
to another. I have my mission — I may
never know it in this life, but I shall be
told it in the next.

I am a link in a chain, a bond of connection
between persons. He has not
created me for naught. I shall do good.
I shall do His work. I shall be an angel
of peace, a preacher of truth in my own
place while not intending it — if I do but
keep His Commandments.

Whatever, wherever I am, I can never be
thrown away. If I am in sickness, my
sickness may serve Him; in perplexity,
my perplexity may serve Him; If I am
in sorrow, my sorrow may serve Him.
He does nothing in vain. He knows what
He is about. He may take away my
friends, He may throw me among
strangers, He may make me feel desolate,
may make my spirits sink, hide my
future from me — still He knows what He
is about. Therefore, I will trust Him.

— from *The Catholic Faith Handbook for Youth.* Reprinted here with
permission of St. Mary's Press. www.smp.org

ACKNOWLEDGMENTS

To the following, with deeply felt gratitude, and without whom I would not be able to live a normal life:

To the late Dr. Lyman Wynne, who correctly diagnosed my disease, bipolar disorder, and took care of me for almost a decade.

To Dr. Joseph Messina, who helped me to live with my disease honestly and courageously.

To Dr. Victoria Korth, who helped me to cope with this disease in a caring manner.

To Kate Schroeder-Bruce, who supports me with a frank and honest approach in accepting and living with bipolar disorder.

To the numerous medical personnel who took care of me while I was hospitalized.

There are many others who directly or indirectly helped me to write this book, and I wish to express my appreciation and gratitude to all of them:

To my editor, Nina Alvarez, who helped me to rewrite many, many pages of my book.

To Flo Smith, an instructor at the Osher Learning Center at RIT, who taught me how to write a memoir and edited some of my stories.

To my many family and friends who read my manuscript and helped me in writing my memoir. I value their friendship and help for a lifetime.

ABOUT THE AUTHOR

Giovanna Campomizzi May is an Italian American immigrant with bipolar disorder. She was a middle school science teacher for sixteen years, during which time she was honored in the Teacher Recognition Program by Canandaigua National Bank & Trust. She also served as the religious formation coordinator with St. Thomas the Apostle Catholic Church. An excerpt from her memoir was published in *As You Were: The Military Review*. Giovanna has a master's degree in education and lives in Rochester, New York, with her husband, Bill. They have three children and six grandchildren.

Made in the USA
Middletown, DE
22 August 2020

16088458R00132